The Agile Manager's Guide To

CUSTOMER-FOCUSED
SELLING

The Agile Manager's Guide To

CUSTOMER-FOCUSED SELLING

SECOND EDITION EXPANDED

By Len D'Innocenzo and Jack Cullen

Velocity Business Publishing
Bristol, Vermont USA

To the Donnas—
Thanks for all your support over the years

Velocity Business Publishing publishes authoritative works of the highest quality. It is not, however, in the business of offering professional, legal, or accounting advice. Each company has its own circumstances and needs, and state and national laws may differ with respect to issues affecting you. If you need legal or other advice pertaining to your situation, secure the services of a professional.

If you'd like additional copies of this book or a catalog of books in the Agile Manager Series®, please get in touch.

- **Write us:**
  Velocity Business Publishing, Inc.
  15 Main Street
  Bristol, VT 05443 USA

- **Call or fax us:**
  1-888-805-8600 in North America (toll-free)
  1-802-453-6669 from all other countries
  1-802-453-2164 (fax)

- **E-mail us:**
  action@agilemanager.com

- **Visit our Web site:**
  www.agilemanager.com

To get in touch with Jack Cullen or Len D'Innocenzo, call 1-978-474-8657 or visit their Web site, www.CRKInteractive.com.

Contents

Books in the Agile Manager Series™:

The Agile Manager's Guide To

CUSTOMER-FOCUSED
SELLING

The Sales Professional Makes the Difference

The Agile Sales Manager was at a Caribbean Resort with the top twenty salespeople in his organization. They were on their sales-incentive trip, President's Club, to celebrate the outstanding job they did the prior fiscal year and to kick off the new year.

After the awards banquet, held on the third night of a seven-day trip, the group got together at the pool-side bar for a nightcap. The Agile Manager quickly found himself cornered by his people. They were on a mission.

Their message to the Agile Sales Manager: The company's product line had become much like that of all the other competitors. One said, "The competition has simply caught up. There's no way to differentiate ourselves any more."

Another said, "Can't you go to the folks in product development, engineering, and marketing and get them to do something? We need to create a sense of urgency before we start heading downhill!"

Everyone nodded in agreement—they didn't want customers to view the product line as "Me, too."

Last call came and went and the Agile Manager walked to his room slowly, thinking about how concerned his troops seemed to be.

Everyone spent the next day shopping. As all the award winners got off the bus and headed into the brightly colored shops that lined the street, the Agile Manager looked across the road towards the ocean. On the beach he saw what appeared to be an open-air market underneath palm trees swaying gently in the tropical breeze.

Curiosity got the best of him, and he decided to check things out away from the crowds. As he walked toward the vendors, he noticed two giant ocean liners out in the crystal clear, blue-green water. Waves splashed gently on the immaculate white-sand beach.

The market had four rows with five blankets spread out in each row to exhibit the items for sale. The Agile Manager was amazed to see that the twenty or so vendors were selling the exact same thing—bananas! As he strolled, he began to smile.

Seeing the Agile Manager approach, one man got up from a chair and shoved a banana in his face. The Agile Manager declined. Another vendor, reading a magazine, never bothered to look up. Several salespeople were busy listening to music through headphones, while others napped or chatted with each other.

Several vendors asked the Agile Manager if he wanted to buy a banana. He said "no" to each.

As he was getting close to finishing his walk, one gentlemen with a big straw hat got up from his chair and greeted him with a smile and handshake. "Hello," said the vendor. "My name is James. I saw you get off the bus across the street. I want to thank you for taking the time to come over here to our market." The Agile Manager noticed a gleam in James's eyes.

"I see from the name on your bus that you are staying at one of our finest resorts," continued James. "How are you enjoying your stay?" The Agile Manager told him and was soon engaged in a pleasant conversation. James asked about restaurants he'd eaten at, where he'd played golf, and which sights he'd seen. After answering each question, James offered useful advice.

Regarding shopping, for instance, James said, "Watch out for the imitation brand-name products sold in the stores across the street. And by the way, pottery is a specialty of our island. Here's the name of a shop that sells the best. It's run by my sister. Mention me and she'll be happy to show you items that may be of special interest to you as gifts or treats for yourself."

James concluded by saying, "I really want to thank you once again for taking the time to come to our market. We are very proud of many things on the island, like our friendly people, beautiful beaches, clean water, and of course our produce. And of all the produce we grow, we are most proud of our bananas."

"Sir," he continued, "could I interest you in trying one of our bananas?"

With a big grin, the Agile Manager said, "Of course. In fact, I'll take two dozen if you'll put a banana on every seat in the bus across the street."

They completed the transaction, and James carried the two bunches of bananas on his shoulders to the bus. All the competing vendors paid close attention, wondering how James had made the sale.

Several hours later, the Agile Manager's salespeople came back with their shopping bags full. They all looked quizzically at the bananas lying on the seats.

On the ride back to the hotel, the Agile Manager used the bus microphone to relate his experience on the beach. To tie the incident to the previous night's conversation, he ended by saying, "So what's the major point of differentiation between us and our competitors? Simple—it's you," he said looking at a woman. "And you and you and you," he said fixing on a different face each time. "The sales professional always makes the difference!"

Although products seem the same, features may look alike, and prices may be very close, all things are never equal. Either positively or negatively, the salesperson makes the difference in the mind of the potential customer.

Why? Because many people buy on emotion. Then they justify or rationalize the decision with logic later on.

We believe that people buy in this order:

1. You, the salesperson.
2. Your company.
3. Your solution, product, or service.

That being the case, effective salespeople sell in the same order:

1. Themselves.
2. Their company.
3. Their solution, product, or service.

When the prospective customer doesn't "buy" the salesperson, the story about the company, product, and services is never heard. Thus, the sales professional must ensure that the message is heard by first gaining emotional acceptance from the potential customer.

Sometimes the product is rich with benefit-laden features and the company producing it is an industry leader.

Yet if the salesperson can't sell him- or herself, the buyer decides to go elsewhere.

That's why sales professionals must accept responsibility for a lost sale. Too many times, salespeople believe they lost a sale because:

- The price was too high;
- The product didn't perform as well as the competitor's;
- The product lacked options customers need;
- The competition bought the business through extreme price breaks.

None of these reasons wash, because customers do business with people they like, trust, and believe to be credible.

Sell Yourself—and the Right Solution

As you'll see, outstanding salespeople make certain the solution they recommend meets the needs and wants of the customer. Good salespeople even pass on an opportunity if they know it's in the best interest of the customer to do so.

Offering the right solution to a problem builds trust and helps prospects buy the salesperson on an emotional level.

And when they do that, they look for reasons to do business with the salesperson's company or avoid doing business with competitors.

What's more, once they "buy" a salesperson, they'll go out of their way to tell others about their experience.

The lesson? **The sales professional makes the difference!**

The rest of this book is about being that professional.

Note: All the stories in this book come straight out of our experience as salesmen and sales managers.

Chapter One

Plan to Establish Trust

The Agile Sales Manager was working in the field with Barry, a successful sales rep. Today they were visiting several large customers to say "thank you" for past business and to strengthen relationships. Barry was one of the top producers in the company. He'd been near the top of the rankings for the past six years, and he finished #1 last year.

The Agile Manager enjoyed working with Barry because of his experience and professionalism, and because of his ability to produce consistently.

The first meeting scheduled was with a large, loyal customer. Their main contact, Dan, had been the vice president of procurement for the past ten years.

On the ride over, Barry said, "Dan is one of the best customers I've ever done business with."

"Why?" asked the Agile Manager.

Barry responded, "Dan is easygoing and trusts me. And I really like him."

The Agile Manager knew how important it is for customers to trust the salesperson. He was curious why Dan trusted Barry; he hoped he had time to ask. Some salespeople are never able to establish trust, and most take lots of time to develop it.

Just before entering the building, Barry told the Agile Manager that Dan was planning to retire next year. He had been with this company for forty-one years, starting as a stock boy and working up through the ranks.

Dan's secretary met them in the lobby and escorted them to Dan's spacious office. As they entered, Dan said, "Barry, good to see you! Is this your manager?"

Barry replied, "Hi, Dan. Yes, this is my sales manager. I'm glad you two are finally getting a chance to meet." They shook hands all around and Dan pointed to the sofa and chairs and motioned for them to sit down. He then poured coffee into two fine china cups.

Dan said, "I've had my coffee quota for the day already. The doctor said one cup a day is all I should have."

"I hope you're still following the doctor's orders," said Barry. "You don't want to go back to the hospital again like last year."

"No, I don't," replied Dan. "I've followed his orders to the letter."

Barry glanced over at the Agile Manager and said, "Dan had an operation last year to repair a blocked artery. He was out of work for four weeks."

The Agile Manager asked, "How are you doing now, Dan?"

"Just as good as new."

Just then one of Dan's managers walked in and said, "Excuse me, Dan. May I interrupt?"

"You just did, Ralph. What is it?"

"Could I borrow Barry for ten minutes? I have the marketing people in my office and we need his advice for the fall lineup."

Dan said, "Barry, do you mind?"

"Not at all. Besides, it will give you two a chance to talk privately for a few minutes."

"Thanks a lot, Barry," said Dan. "Come back when you're done."

After they left the office, the Agile Manager asked Dan, "How long has Barry been your sales rep?"

"About eight years," replied Dan. "Our people think Barry's the best salesman they work with."

"Why do you say that?" asked the Agile Manager.

"Because they trust Barry. He tells the truth and they can always depend on him," said Dan.

"I see," said the Agile Manager, nodding his head.

As Lou Holtz* says in his speeches and in his bestselling video *Do Right with Lou Holtz,* there are three unasked questions people have when they meet other people:

1. Can I trust you?
2. Are you committed?
3. Do you care about me?

The answers to these three questions are basic. Yet they are often overlooked, if not ignored, by average salespeople. The answers to the three unasked questions are:

- Always do what's right.
- Always do your best.
- Always treat others as *they'd* like to be treated.

Note that you don't answer the questions with words, but with actions. When you do that, potential customers will "buy" you, the salesperson, at an emotional level.

Earn Trust

Trust is the cornerstone of any business relationship. Without it, there's no sale. And if customers don't trust a salesperson, they rarely say so. Instead, they say things like, "We're happy with our present supplier," or "That's not a priority with us right now; call back in six months," or "Leave us some literature and we'll get back to you."

All of these are stalls or smoke screens from a potential customer, and all are usually the result of a lack of trust. If a customer doesn't trust a salesperson, he never says, "I don't trust you. We're not interested." Instead, he's nonconfrontational and

---

*Take a look at Lou's book *Winning Every Day.* Many of the messages in it and in his video are of particular relevance to sales professionals.

says things to put the salesperson off as nicely as he can.

Trust is one of the most difficult things to establish, and one of the easiest things to lose.

And you can't create trust by saying, "Don't worry—you can trust me." You have to earn trust. You earn the trust of customers by doing the right things: being honest and open, doing what you say you will, treating others with respect. Professional salespeople look for ways to prove they are trustworthy.

One way to do that: During your initial exchange, do more listening than talking. Use open-ended questions (who, what, where, why, and how) and probes (tell me, please explain, etc.). These will solicit thoughtful responses.

Show Commitment

The second unasked question is, "Are you committed?" It, too, is vitally important. Customers need to know they are dealing with a professional, someone who will deal with them honestly, stand behind the product or service, and stick around after the sale.

Building the trust that shows your commitment to prospects requires effort. To build trust:

1. Get in Step (Pace). First, you need to communicate with people on the same channel. The secret to getting on the same wavelength is to find common ground with your prospects. You need to get in step with their pace.

Best Tip
Look for ways to prove you are trustworthy. Your customers and prospects are looking for reasons to trust you.

To do this, consider—before meaningful communications begin—how they think, act, speak, and feel. Listen carefully to what your customers or prospects say and what they imply. Observe how people act and what's going on in their surroundings.

Then do what superior salespeople do quite naturally: Place

prospects or customers at ease by getting in step with their rate of speech, mood, feelings, body language, and even beliefs.

Is it possible for you to share all the beliefs your customers or prospects have? No, it is unlikely you will agree with everything your prospects believe in. But it is possible to find some common ground with each customer or prospect you contact. This is called diplomacy.

Another way of getting in step with your prospects is to show a sincere interest in them. If they like you and feel you really want to help them, they will be more willing to let you. Demonstrate your sincerity by asking about their goals and needs. Don't assume you already know them.

|Best **T**ip

Treat others as they'd like to be treated. This shows you care about them.

2. Show Proof. Professional salespeople are committed to being of maximum benefit to customers. They can show that they've helped customers—that they are *committed* to serving customers—by providing proof sources that include not just reference names and numbers but also testimonial letters. (How do you get a testimonial letter showing your commitment to a customer's success? Ask for it!)

And customers who write testimonial letters for you will actively suggest to friends and associates that you could be of service to them. That sends a message to the people they speak to: You are not only committed to excellence but you really care about your customers.

3. Provide Credentials. Just as applying for a job demands a résumé, selling to a new customer requires credentials. Credentials lead to credibility, and credibility leads to trust.

Create a résumé for yourself. Outline your education, previous employment, honors and awards, special training, professional and civic organizations you belong to, and your hobbies or interests.

Show Them You Care

To get people to "buy" you, show them you care. How? Here's a simple method: Sell people the products and services they *need* instead of selling them what you have.

As simple as this sounds, salespeople too often sell what they have instead of finding out what prospects need.

Stop selling and start helping customers. Distribute those golden testimonial letters that show the value you've provided.

It'll be obvious to prospects that your customers cared enough to help you because you came through for them.

Dan went on, "Barry is probably the best salesperson I've done business with in my forty-one years here."

"That's really interesting," said the Agile Manager. "Why do you say that?"

"Because," said Dan, "Barry does two things that make him different from all the other salespeople I've worked with."

"What are they?"

"They're both very important," said Dan. "You might want to write these down and tell all your salespeople."

The Agile Manager opened his notebook and took out a pen to record Dan's words of wisdom.

"Number one," said Dan forcefully, "Barry really cares about his customers."

The Agile Manager scribbled "Barry cares" in the notebook and said, "Tell me more."

"Sure," Dan replied. "Barry is different because he doesn't say he cares with words. He proves he cares by his actions. Let me give you an example. Last year when I was in the hospital, I received lots of cards and flowers from salespeople. I even had a few come visit me at the hospital during the day. I think they put me down on their call reports for the day. One guy in particular was just concerned about when I was coming back to work. It was like he wanted to make sure I didn't croak!" Dan laughed.

He went on, "Well, Barry was different. He came by five or

six times over the four weeks I was in the hospital or at home recuperating. And not during the day. Barry visited me at night or on the weekend when he could have been with his family. He even brought over a casserole and an apple pie his wife cooked."

"Wow," said the Agile Manager. "That's impressive."

"You bet," said Dan. "Barry really does care, like the good friend he is. His actions speak louder than words."

"Yes, they do," replied the Agile Manager. "What was the second thing, Dan?"

"Oh, yeah," replied Dan. "The second thing Barry does that makes him different is that he always makes sure we get what we need."

The Agile Manager wrote, "Makes sure they get what they need."

Dan continued: "I can't tell you how many times my people ask Barry for his advice on a project they're working on. He knows our business and he usually knows what we need. And your company doesn't sell everything we require. Barry tells us if he can't supply what we need in the time frame we need it, and he'll recommend a place or two we can get it."

"Does he ever turn business away?" asked the Agile Manager.

"Only when your people can't meet our delivery date. Barry makes sure we get what we need when we need it."

The Agile Manager looked directly in Dan's eyes and said, "The two items you mentioned are very important. But haven't any other salespeople shown they care and made sure you got what you've needed over the years?"

Dan smiled and said, "Sure, when it suited them. Barry's the only salesperson who does those two things every day!"

The Agile Manager smiled broadly, nodded approval, and said, "Barry is one of the best."

Just then Barry walked in and said, "How are the two of you doing?"

"We're doing just fine," said Dan. "We've had a good talk. Your ears should be burning," chuckled Dan.

"Oh, talking behind my back are you?" said Barry.

The Agile Manager said, "Dan's been telling me why he and the others here like doing business with you."

"Really?" replied Barry. "What did he say?"

"Oh, I just told your boss why we like you so much. You owe me big time!"

The Agile Manager said, "Dan's shared with me a very important lesson that all our salespeople should learn."

Barry said, "What's that?"

"That salespeople *earn* trust through their actions and not their words, and when you establish credibility, then trust, people enjoy doing business with you."

"You bet," said Dan.

"That's really nice, Dan. Thanks," said Barry.

"Don't mention it," replied Dan. "You earned it."

The Agile Manager added, "Thank you very much, Dan. I came in today to thank you for your business. We really do appreciate it. Thanks, too, for the lessons in salesmanship. I'll make sure all my people hear about it."

With that Barry said, "I'm afraid we need to go now or we'll be late for our next meeting. Is that OK with you, Dan?"

"No problem," replied Dan. "Wait a minute, I've got something for you, Barry."

"What is it—an order?" quipped Barry.

"No, not today, Barry," said Dan. "It's those Cubs tickets I promised your son. They play the Dodgers on Saturday, remember."

Barry said, "He's asked me almost every day, Dan, if you really had season's tickets."

The Agile Manager could not remain silent. "Wait a minute. Isn't the salesperson supposed to be the one giving the tickets?"

Barry and Dan laughed.

"Barry's son loves the Cubs," said Dan, "and I've had these tickets for years. There's nothing better than a father and son going to Wrigley Field on a warm, sunny day. Have a hot dog for me!" Dan looked at Barry with genuine affection.

They shook hands and as they walked away, the Agile Manager thought to himself, What a great example of credibility and trust to talk about at the sales meeting next month.

Remember: Facts alone seldom result in gaining customers. If they don't first trust you or if you lack credibility, you won't get the sale. Focus on gaining a customer, not just getting an order.

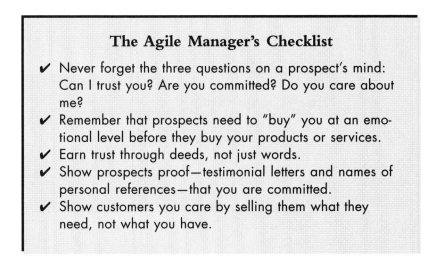

The Agile Manager's Checklist

✔ Never forget the three questions on a prospect's mind: Can I trust you? Are you committed? Do you care about me?

✔ Remember that prospects need to "buy" you at an emotional level before they buy your products or services.

✔ Earn trust through deeds, not just words.

✔ Show prospects proof—testimonial letters and names of personal references—that you are committed.

✔ Show customers you care by selling them what they need, not what you have.

Chapter Two

Learn to *Really* Listen

Think about your best friend. Picture that person in your mind's eye. Now, with that person in mind, think about *why* you regard him or her as your best friend. What is it about this person that leads you to feel the way that you do?

Take a minute or two to answer those questions.

There is a good chance that among the many things you value in your very best friend, one stands out: That person really listens to you. Simply put, he or she is a good listener. Someone you can tell about your problems, dilemmas, opportunities, challenges—things that are important, maybe even critical, to you.

Further, it's likely this person isn't quick to pass judgment on you, either. He actually listens to all you have to say, and doesn't just look for the chance to jump in and tell you what he'd do if he were you. He may serve as a solid sounding board that you feel comfortable with when looking for advice or when you need a place to unload your thoughts.

Either way, no matter what he does after listening, you're glad he was there for you. You trust him. You feel safe, emotionally, with the fact that he knows what you are thinking.

It's the Same in Sales

Really listening—and letting prospective customers know you are really listening—is also critical in earning the trust that encourages customers to provide the valuable information you need to be of service or assistance to them.

Just because you ask good questions doesn't guarantee your answers are going to be meaningful. They won't be, in fact, unless you listen well. Doing so helps earn the trust of customers and enhances your credibility.

Best Tip

Listen really, really well. It's a key ingredient in earning customers for life.

Listening well, in fact, can put you in a different class of salespeople—those who have customers for life.

Let People Know You're Listening

There once was a brilliant fellow with the ability to carry out several activities simultaneously. He had no difficulty listening to someone while also reading, writing, or even drawing. How productive he was! That strength, however, became a weakness.

Imagine how a client felt telling this fellow about her organization's future business direction. While she shares the most confidential of plans, this guy doodles or glances at the *Wall Street Journal.*

No matter how skilled at listening he was, he sent a message to clients that said, "My doodling or reading is more important to me right now than you are." Or, "I'm so smart that I can seem to be ignoring you."

It's not enough to just listen. Your customers need to know they are being listened to and understood.

One day, the Agile Sales Manager was in Pittsburgh working with a salesman from one of his firm's Value-Added Resellers (VARs). This particular VAR sold several types of computer systems, including those from the Agile Manager's company.

The salesman, Harry, appeared to be thirty-two or thirty-three years old. He was meeting with a growing CPA firm that used a computer manufactured by the Agile Manager's company, so he invited him along. The firm was planning to double its network of computers, and Harry wanted the order. It would be worth more than $200,000.

While they waited in the lobby of the CPA firm, the Agile Manager listened to Harry explain how he expected to get the approval today. Harry said the CPA firm was twenty years old and had just merged with a smaller firm. This added both clients and staff, which would require more computing power.

The Agile Manager noticed several fine leather chairs, mahogany tables, tasteful paintings, and even a sculpture. This was, indeed, the office of an established and very profitable company.

Within a few minutes a distinguished-looking gentleman in his early sixties appeared and introduced himself as Bob Gray, one of the partners in the firm. He asked Harry and the Agile Manager to follow him into a small conference room just off the lobby.

As they entered the conference room, Harry asked Bob how long he'd been associated with the firm. Bob replied he was a CPA and one of the founders. Harry nodded and said, "Well, it looks like business is going very well for you."

Bob replied, "Yes, business has been very good. We've grown each year since we began, and with this latest merger, we're now one of the largest public accounting firms in the city."

"That's why we're here today Bob," said Harry. "As you know, your assistant called and asked us to stop over to discuss how you could add more computers. I think he said you needed to just about double what you now have."

"Yes. We need to add another hundred systems over the next few months," said Bob.

Harry quickly replied, "You've purchased from our company in the past, and things seemed to have worked out well. We appreciate your coming back to us now that you need more systems."

"Did you bring the information my assistant asked you for

regarding configurations, pricing, and delivery?" asked Bob.

"Yes, I have it here," said Harry. "Shall we review it?"

For the next twenty minutes Harry did all the talking. He explained to Bob the latest product enhancements dealing with processor speed, memory, storage disk capacity, internal modems, and graphical user interfaces. Harry knew his products well. He literally became a "talking brochure."

Surprisingly to the Agile Manager, Bob seemed very interested in these specifics. He listened intently, leaning over the conference table reading the literature Harry had placed in front of him.

Then Harry reviewed the pricing page he had been asked to bring with him. Once again, Harry did most of the talking. Bob only asked two questions—one to clarify how the quantity discount would work and another confirming payment terms of net 30 days.

The Agile Manager thought Harry was about to close a very large sale. Harry took a deep breath, and the Agile Manager expected him to ask for the order.

Wrong!

Harry said, "Bob, let me tell you about our leasing option."

Bob shook his head and said, "No, thank you." The Agile Manager heard Bob, but Harry wasn't listening. Instead, he was busy taking a leasing folder out of his briefcase. Harry told Bob he would like to explain some of the benefits of leasing.

Best Tip

Remember: You have to listen well to ask good questions. And asking good questions is the only way you can provide customers with valuable solutions.

Thinking that Harry simply didn't hear Bob say no, the Agile Manager said, "Harry, I don't think Bob is interested in leasing."

"Bob, this will just take a few minutes. Then you can decide if leasing is an option you'd like to consider," responded Harry. The next three minutes seemed like an hour. Harry discussed how leasing would save working capital for the firm because it could spread out payments and not have to pay cash up front.

He launched into a review of a three-year leasing plan he was proposing and discussed two buyout options that were included as part of the package.

Bob sat upright in his chair with his arms folded. He looked at the Agile Manager, sending very negative body language. Harry wasn't listening to Bob. Bob finally slapped his hands on the conference table and said, in a loud, agitated voice, "Enough! This meeting is over. I told you I'm a CPA. I know the benefits of leasing. At this firm, we pay cash! Good day to you both."

Bob stood up, opened the door to the conference room, and walked out.

Finally, Harry stopped talking. Like a deer frozen by the headlights of an approaching automobile, he just stared at the open door. Harry turned to the Agile Manager and said, "What did I say?"

"You talked yourself right out of the sale because you weren't listening, Harry," said the Agile Manager. "You didn't hear Bob say 'no thank you' to leasing."

On the ride back to the office the Agile Manager decided to do a little "curbside coaching." He told Harry he did a good job of explaining the new products, and the pricing and delivery options. He then asked Harry what he felt went wrong. Harry said, "You mentioned that I didn't listen."

"That's right," said the Agile Manager. "What did you hear about Bob's background with the firm?"

"What do you mean?" asked Harry.

"Bob told you he was one of the founders of the firm and a CPA himself," the Agile Manager pointed out. "That should tell you something about his knowledge of finance options. Then,

---

A Salesperson's 'Don'ts'

1. Don't be too judgmental.
2. Don't explain too early or too often.
3. Don't interrupt.
4. Don't sound or appear challenging, hostile, or insincere.

you started talking about the benefits of leasing, without asking Bob if leasing was something he would be interested in. I thought you didn't hear Bob say 'no, thank you' so I repeated what he said to you. But you didn't hear what I was saying, either. You were on a roll and wanted to tell Bob, the CPA, the benefits of leasing."

Best Tip

When meeting a potential customer for the first time, listen twice as much as you speak.

"You must think I'm pretty dumb," said Harry. Not wanting to kick Harry when he was down, the Agile Manager said, "I'm sure you've had better days. You were probably excited because you thought you had the sale locked up. Maybe you thought giving them finance options would help you close the sale? I don't know why you went off on leasing like that, but Bob sure came apart like a cheap watch. Anyway, you're not alone. Lots of salespeople don't listen as well as they should."

"I thought I was a good listener. Obviously I was wrong. How can I become a better listener?" asked Harry.

"Here are some things to consider to become a better listener, Harry," said the Agile Manager. A good coaching session was in progress.

A good number of salespeople had people say to them, "You should go into sales. You're a really good talker—you have a real gift of gab."

But once in the profession, wise salespeople realize a key to success lies in their ability to be effective, active listeners. They learn to interpret and respond to verbal messages and other cues, like body language, in ways that are appropriate.

Don't Do All the Talking

It is estimated that people filter out or change the intended meaning of what they hear in 70 percent of all communications.

Top salespeople don't fall into that category. The best of the best are far more concerned and interested in the ideas, thoughts, and feelings of others. They are very comfortable listening to their prospects and customers.

Less-skilled salespeople—the majority—tend to dominate the discussion by doing most of the talking. That's why the image of the fast-talking, glib salesperson is so firmly rooted in the mind of the public.

When given the choice, most of us prefer to buy from and do business with people we like. Who do we like? People who make us feel comfortable, especially people who are genuinely interested in what we have to say.

Invest Time in Listening

Listening will help you establish credibility and build trust. That is why it is so critical for you to invest the majority of your time listening in an initial meeting with prospects. Prospective customers will like a salesperson who listens intently rather than one who just runs off at the mouth. The reason is simple: When you listen to a person, you build up his or her self-esteem.

Of course, you can probably think of a few people whose self-esteem is already off the charts! Surely they don't care about more chances to express themselves, right? Wrong! It doesn't matter what self-image one has. Your active listening, in a sincere way that is genuinely caring, will make people feel good about themselves.

Best Tip

Provide feedback when listening to prospects or customers. It shows them that you're really listening.

The salesperson who talks too much and listens poorly is on the fast track to annoying, irritating, and alienating both prospects and customers. You see, in the minds of prospects and customers, if you're not listening to them, you're ignoring them. The message: You don't value what they think.

Now some salespeople do make an effort to uncover a prospect's thoughts, problems, and opinions by asking good ques-

---

Sales Professional's Hot Tip #1

Improve Your Listening. Customers are comfortable with and trusting of salespeople who are excellent listeners. To listen better:

1. Prepare questions in advance.

2. Tell customers that, to be of the most help to them and to gain understanding, you'll initially listen twice as much as you talk. And keep that commitment—you'll be a breath of fresh air.

3. Maintain comfortable eye contact.

4. Lean toward your customer. People judge if you're listening by your body language. Don't send the wrong signal by slouching down in a chair while a customer is describing, with emotion, a problem. Be engaged by leaning forward in your chair.

5. Use the customer's name.

6. Provide good feedback by paraphrasing what you hear and asking clarifying questions when needed. Customers will feel more confident if they're sure you understand their situation.

7. Take written notes. (Ask permission first.) Customers will appreciate it, and they will emphasize key points as they speak. Also, they may slow down their speech rate.

8. Concentrate on your customers or your mind may wander. You don't want to send a message that you're ignoring them.

---

tions. However, people will be put off if their answers aren't really being listened to. Worse yet, they'll be angry or hurt if they feel they aren't being heard and understood.

We've seen far too many instances where salespeople have committed major mistakes by interrupting others in the middle of their sentences or thoughts. Resist the temptation to jump in even if you have some wonderful pearls of wisdom to share and enlighten them with. They'll be offended when you cut them off with, "I know what you mean . . ." Your words will only fall on deaf ears anyway.

Customers Buy on Emotion

People usually make a decision to buy based on emotions. Then they support that decision with logic. That's why a prospect's perception that you're listening affects his or her decision to buy or not.

To avoid the pitfalls the average salesperson falls into, take a few minutes to go back over the last few pages. You'll see that we've been addressing things that involve emotions all along.

In selling yourself, then, first listen to a prospective customer. Let his initial emotional feelings about the process be positive. Nothing gets the prospect's emotions involved faster, one way or the other, than the perception that you're listening.

Practice Self-Discipline

To be an outstanding listener, you must possess strong self-discipline. Why is this so? Because the average individual speaks at a rate of only 125 to 150 words per minute. Yet we can, on average, listen at a rate up to four times faster than that—500 to 600 words per minute!

The bottom line is that you have two-thirds of your listening time free or available to you to let your mind wander to think about other things. Sales professionals have to be on their guards to concentrate on the prospect or customer. You must stay focused. And your prospects and customers are smart—they'll know in various ways, including body language, that you've drifted off on other things. It takes strength of character to maintain your focus when listening.

Best Tip

Do what's right for your customer. A long-term relationship is a lot more profitable than one quick sale.

If you follow our advice, you'll find that the prospective customer will provide you with the information you need to be of greatest service. If you've invested the majority of the time initially trying to understand the thoughts, problems, opportunities, goals, issues, and needs of the prospect, you'll see a big return on that investment. People will be more receptive to the ideas and solutions you have to help them get what they want.

When they compare your presentation to that of another salesperson who doesn't listen as well, they may evaluate both analytically, but they'll empathize with you emotionally. They'll be more receptive and appreciative of your proposals because they first made an emotional decision to "buy you." They know you understand the situation and believe you genuinely care more about assisting them than other salespeople who just talk too much.

And, by the way, they're right.

The Agile Manager's Checklist

✔ Listen well. It's critical to earning the trust that results in long-term relationships with customers.

✔ Let people know you're listening by offering feedback and visual cues.

✔ Remember: When customers know they're being listened to and understood, they'll reward you with sales.

✔ Talk less. You'll do a better job hearing what your customers are telling you through their words and their body language.

✔ Best advice: *Invest* your time in listening.

Chapter Three

Create Interest

The Agile Sales Manager was meeting with one of the newest sales reps on the team, Jane, to review prospects. There weren't very many, which is often the case when new salespeople take over a territory.

One of Jane's prospects did look interesting, however. It was a large company with operations in over one hundred countries.

The Agile Manager asked, "Where are you with the International account?"

"Nowhere," responded Jane. "I can't get anyone to return my calls."

"What level are you calling?" inquired the Agile Manager.

"I've got the name of a middle-level manager at the home office," said Jane. "I had good luck approaching prospects at that level last quarter. I figured it worked before, so I'd try it again."

"There was a story about this company in the trade press last week. Did you see it?"

"Yes," said Jane. "I've got it right here. They have a new vice president of sales for their North American operations. He was quoted in the story."

"Very good," said the Agile Manager. "Have you thought about calling on him or writing an approach letter? New executives present excellent prospecting opportunities—they're eager to make an impact."

"Isn't he too busy to want to speak with me?" asked Jane. "I never seem to capture the interest of senior-level executives. They're busy with more important things than to talk with me about our services and products."

"You're exactly right!" said the Agile Manager. "They are much too busy to talk to salespeople trying to sell something."

Jane looked puzzled. "Then I should not approach at the executive level, right?"

"Wrong," said the Agile Manager, "You should definitely approach at the executive level. But to capture the executive's interest, you have to talk about things the executive is interested in." Jane still looked confused.

"If you want to create interest with a sales v.p.," continued the Agile Manager, "think like a sales v.p. Talk about things sales v.p.'s are interested in."

"How can you know what they're interested in?" asked Jane.

"We don't know all the things sales v.p.'s are interested in, but you can be sure they are interested in things like increasing sales productivity and profit margins, improving customer satisfaction, opening new markets, gaining competitive advantages, and reducing the sales-cycle time.

"Now," the Agile Manager continued, "do you think any of our products or services can help a sales v.p. achieve any of these things?"

"Yes," said Jane enthusiastically. "Most of them."

"Well," said the Agile Manager, "to create interest, then, talk about what we have helped our customers do, instead of what we sell. It's more interesting and—who knows—you may get lucky and strike a chord with that new sales v.p. at International Company.

Jane asked, "Should I call him on the phone or send a letter?"

"Whichever way you're more comfortable," replied the Agile Manager. "Both are effective. Given the busy schedule of top executives, a letter outlining the type of results we can provide followed by a telephone call may be best."

"That makes sense. I'll give it a try."

"Just make sure you write clearly, briefly, and put your bottom line—your most important idea or benefit—right up front," said the Agile Manager. "And I suggest you mention one or two of our customers who have written us testimonial letters. They'll add credibility and help differentiate your letter from others. Also, make sure you ask for something specific, like an opportunity to meet him in person."

"Great idea," said the sales rep. "I'll get started as soon as we finish. Do you think I should include any literature?"

"Only general information about our company. Avoid product literature, because you don't know what they need yet," said the Agile Manager. "All you want to do is create enough interest so you can 'sell' an appointment. You could include a few copies of testimonial letters or a list of references. Again, this will help establish credibility and differentiate your letter from the others."

"I'll let you know what happens," said Jane.

Too many salespeople chase after low-level prospects who lack buying authority.

Best advice: Approach the person who can say yes or no, regardless of how anyone else in the company feels about it. This person has the power, influence, and authority for the bottom line. The buck stops in her office!

Also, too many salespeople talk about what they're selling rather than talking about things of interest to your prospect. In general, prospects will be most interested in buying if:

- You can improve the manner in which employees deal with customers and business partners;
- Your product, service, or solution will improve employee productivity;
- Your product, service, or solution helps the firm gain a competitive advantage;
- Your product, service, or solution will fatten the bottom line.

A solution, by the way, can include one or more products, services, programs, contractual approaches, and recommended implementations.

How do you identify the person to contact? Simply ask your-self, "Who has responsibility, power, authority, and influence in the organization?"

Make Prospecting a Daily Habit

Wise salespeople look for new business opportunities today, no matter how well things are going, to replace business they may lose tomorrow.

First, devote time to looking for new opportunities within your existing customer base. Next, go after companies that do not use your products, services, or solutions. Finally, target accounts that do business with a competitor.

Prospecting requires time and effort from sales representatives already busy with their daily routines. Nonetheless, prospecting for additional opportunities and opening new accounts is a high priority for any sales professional. Consider it an investment!

To be effective, prospecting must be done each day. Wise salespeople turn existing customers into active references and leverage past successes into new business.

Best Tip

When prospecting, aim high. Approach the person who can say 'yes' or 'no' to the product or service you are offering—regardless of what anyone else says.

Use This Seven-Point Prospecting System

All successful salespeople have a system for finding prospects and turning them into customers. Here's one of the best:

1. Identify your top three sources for quality leads. Sales professionals use two kinds of sources for leads:

People Sources
- Your current customers
- Community-service organizations
- Prospects

Sales Professional's Hot Tip #2

Put the Blinders On. The Agile Sales Manager's mind wandered back to an incident in which his first sales manager passed along the best piece of advice he ever received.

It was a few days before the Kentucky Derby, and his manager drew an oval on a piece of paper.

"Imagine that this is the race track at Churchill Downs," he said. "What will be different for the three-year old horses running in this year's Derby?"

"Well," said the young Agile Manager. "They'll run a farther distance than they ever have before—and in front of over 100,000 people."

His mentor smiled and said, "That's right, that's right! I'm glad to see you know something about the racing game. Now, the other unique thing all the horses will experience is what those people in attendance will be doing and where they'll be doing it." He paused and drew people on the outside of the oval.

"You see," he continued, "Thoroughbred horses are accustomed to having people on their right side only as they run a race. That won't change. For this particular race, the throngs of 'rail birds' will be screaming their heads off. So will the more refined set, sitting in the grandstand wearing their suits and fashionable straw hats while sipping mint juleps."

"And how about the ten thousand people that are partying in the infield—many of whom don't even know there is a race taking place!"

The sales manager laughed. "Yep. And those people on the infield, inside the racing circle, will add to the horses' confusion and nervousness by being on their left side. That's why many of the horses will run with a new piece of equipment, and something they may never wear again: blinders. This is to keep them focused and avoid distractions."

The sales chief paused again. "I have watched the Derby for over twenty years and I can tell you that there are always

> **Put the Blinders On, continued**
> some horses wearing blinders for the first time to avoid being
> distracted. Their trainers feel it's the best way for them to get
> from the starting gate to the finish line as fast as they can. It
> keeps their minds on the business at hand." He looked off into
> the distance, then looked directly into the young Agile Man-
> ager's eyes.
>
> "As *your* trainer," he said, "I consider you to be a thorough-
> bred in the sales profession. What's going on in the stands
> and the infield doesn't matter. What matters is that you get to
> the finish line first. Put the blinders on and don't ever take them
> off. That's how you'll win the race."

- Other salespeople
- Professional and personal friends
- Service and support people

Data Sources

- Advertising responses
- Industry trade directories
- Telephone directories/Yellow pages
- Business directories
- Chambers of Commerce
- Newspapers
- Trade shows, seminars
- World Wide Web

Qualifying prospects to fit your company's profile of the ideal
customer will help you be more effective when prospecting. Remember: You don't get rewarded in sales for being busy.

Working with both people and data sources is important in
qualifying opportunities. This gives you leads as well as information to match against predetermined criteria you can put together that describes the ideal prospect company.

Your manager can help you assemble these criteria. Here's a
short list to get you started thinking:

—A new executive has been appointed.

—A merger has taken place.

—The company is growing or downsizing.

—The company is in a highly competitive environment.

—You have a unique solution to an identified need.

2. Have the right information before you make contact. Know about the industry, the company's financial situation, business/market conditions, current environment, problem areas, etc.

3. Know the position or job function of the best people to contact to create interest. Possibilities: president, CEO, COO, VP/general manager, CFO/controller, department managers, etc.

4. Use an effective method to contact these people. Options: phone call, letter, e-mail, fax, or third-party introduction. (The ideal contact method is through a third-party introduction.) If you prefer sending a letter first, indicate you will be calling within five to seven working days. Then be sure to do that.

5. Have methods for getting past the "gatekeeper." Gatekeepers should be treated with respect and courtesy. Many people in these positions are service oriented and accommodating. They can be very helpful if approached the right way.

Remember: Their job is to screen out the unimportant calls. Make your call important. Let them know the reasons for your contact and be sure to state those in terms of benefits to the individual they work with. More on that in point #6.

Also, try calling early or late in the day when the gatekeeper may not be there. At executive levels, you'll have a good "hit rate" of reaching your desired contact directly. Of course, preparation is the key here to ensure you make an immediate, positive impression and capture the prospect's interest. This leads to the next and most crucial point.

Best Tip
A good time to initiate business: when an organization restructures or shuffles jobs.

6. Use your three best initial benefit statements to create

interest. Your initial approach, whether by letter or phone, should have one important objective: to create interest so the contact will invest time with you.

Benefits involve things that increase, improve, gain, grow, maximize, enhance and/or decrease, lower, reduce, minimize, control, and manage.

Provide the prospect with three benefits in an opening paragraph of a letter or within the first thirty seconds of a phone call.

| Best Tip
|
To create interest, develop three ideas that benefited other customers and that you believe will also benefit the prospect's business.

Why three? It'll improve your chances of success. Choose three that will be of interest to someone in that person's position. Do your homework and make the most of the opportunity by addressing areas of importance to the organization or person you approach. (See page 48 for a look at what interests people in particular positions.)

To improve your credibility, mention where you've been of benefit to others. The more specific and relevant the better. For example:

"XYZ Company has worked with us to reduce time to market, gain a competitive advantage, and increase market share."

Then ask for an investment of time. "If you'd invest thirty minutes with me, we could explore how we might help achieve some of your important initiatives. How does that sound?"

7. Have a follow-up system that works—and that you use.

The next week, the Agile Sales Manager received a phone call from Jane. "You'll never guess what just happened," she said excitedly. "I was preparing to follow up on the letter I sent to that v.p. of sales at the International Company when the phone rang. It was him! He called me before I could call him!"

"Great! What did he say?" asked the Agile Manager.

"He wanted to know if we *really* were able to increase sales at one of the reference companies I included. He said he knew the v.p. of sales at that company and was going to call him to check us out."

"That's great," said the Agile Manager. "How did you respond?"

"I asked him if he needed the phone number and said I was glad he was taking the time to check us out. He asked how we were able to increase sales and with what products."

"What did you say?" asked the Agile Manager.

"I told him we craft-customized solutions with our products and services to help our customers achieve specific results," said Jane.

"Good job," said the Agile Manager. "What happened next?"

"Well, he asked me if I thought we could help *him* increase sales," said Jane.

"How did you respond?" asked the Agile Manager.

"I said we wouldn't know for sure until we learned more about his business situation. Then I asked him if he would give me thirty minutes for a face-to-face meeting."

"And what did he say?"

"He said be in his office at 10 A.M. sharp on Friday!" said the rep. "Do you believe how lucky I got?!"

"Luck," said the Agile Manager, "is when preparation meets opportunity. The harder you work, the luckier you get. Good work!"

The Agile Manager's Checklist

✔ Create interest by focusing on areas of interest to the prospect, like:
- Improving employee productivity
- Helping to gain a competitive advantage
- Fattening the bottom line.

✔ Have methods to get beyond the gatekeepers who guard decision makers.

✔ Know who is best to contact for what you're selling (CEO? Department manager? Controller?).

✔ Whenever you can, have a friend or acquaintance introduce you to a prospect.

Chapter Four

Conduct A Customer-Focused Interview

The Agile Sales Manager was planning a sales meeting involving the entire sales team. The company's meeting coordinator did some preliminary legwork by checking out a dozen different hotels. She recommended that the Agile Manager visit three of them in particular.

When he visited the first two, he found that each was very much product-focused in their sales approaches. In both cases, he was greeted by a salesperson in the hotel business office and escorted into a conference room. There, each salesperson asked the same questions: "How many sleeping rooms would you need for your meeting? How many meal functions do you plan on having? Most importantly, when are you planning on having your meeting?"

Three minutes into the first meeting, the hotel sales person disappeared into the back office, checked the calendar, and came back looking as though he had lost a best friend. He said, "Gee, I'm sorry we don't have those dates available. Would you consider changing the dates of your sales meeting?"

"Nope," said the Agile Manager, and he ended the meeting abruptly.

The second meeting ended prematurely for the same reason.

At the third hotel, the Agile Manager found a salesperson who took a completely different approach. "I got a little bit of information about you and your company from your meeting coordinator," she said. "Would you mind confirming some of that information and answering a few more questions?"

The Agile Manager was impressed with the questions she asked, especially the ones about what had worked well and not so well at past sales meetings he'd attended. "What are some of the things that you would like to continue to do or perhaps do differently at this year's event?"

Now here's an effective salesperson, thought the Agile Manager. None of the other two cared about what I believe to be the keys to a successful meeting. And she hasn't even yet asked me about numbers or dates.

The hotel salesperson then said, "From my experience working with other sales executives in planning meetings like this, I know they usually have specific objectives they're trying to achieve. These include things like introducing new compensation plans, announcing new products and programs, or conducting training sessions to increase skills and generate excitement. Are these among the things you are trying to accomplish at this meeting?"

"Yes—all three," said the Agile Manager. "We're introducing new products, holding training sessions, and announcing changes to the compensation plan. But most important, the purpose of the meeting is to kick off the new fiscal year by giving the sales organization a sense of purpose and identity."

He went on to explain that the company had poor sales last year and morale, as well as confidence, was low.

The hotel sales representative asked, "Do you have any specific ideas to address the 'sense of purpose' issue?"

The Agile Manager smiled. "I've decided on a theme for the meeting: 'If you can't run with the Big Dogs, stay on the porch.' I want to give everyone attending a T-shirt with that slogan and a picture of a giant St. Bernard on it when they check in."

"Interesting," said the sales rep. "What's behind that message?"

"I want to convey that, as the people responsible for generat-

---

Sales Professional's Hot Tip #3

Plan Your Day. Time is your greatest asset in business, and managing time well is one of the foundations for sales success. That's because selling is always a race against time—to get in an extra call or two a day or to beat competitors to the punch.

To use your time wisely:

1. Know exactly what you are going to do in the morning.

2. Work by appointment, and make appointments as early in the morning as possible. This tends to get you off to a fast start each day and makes your sales call more professional. It also assures, in most cases, the customer will be in.

3. Review your daily to-do list the night before. Have your to-do list ready to go for the next day.

4. Review your work schedule for the upcoming week each Saturday or Sunday evening.

5. Use Friday afternoons to finalize the next week's schedule.

---

ing revenue, the sales folks are the big dogs, or lead dogs, of the company. I want people to understand that anything less than consistently attaining sales quota is unacceptable."

"Anything else?"

"Well I do want people to have fun and get to know one other during the evenings. But I also want them ready to answer the bell at 7:30 each morning when we kick off meetings."

"So," she said, " 'If you can't run with the Big Dogs, stay on the porch.' I love it. I wish you the best of luck with the slogan at the meeting."

She then asked more about the three main purposes of the meeting and what kind of facilities and services he'd need. As the Agile Manager explained these needs in great detail, she took notes.

When they were finished, she said, "If you are able to achieve your objectives for the meeting, especially the part about meeting and exceeding quota, how significant would that be for you personally?"

"Well," said the Agile Manager, "the company has a bonus plan that pays out if revenue objectives are met during a year. Unfortunately, those bonuses weren't paid last year. If we could turn things around, starting with this kickoff meeting, we'd be on our way to getting those year-end bonuses. Also, in the eyes of everyone else in the company, the salespeople would really earn that 'Big Dog' label."

"I really hope I have an opportunity to work with you on this project," said the salesperson warmly. "If you don't mind, I'd like to confirm some other things that your coordinator told me regarding number of people, number of sleeping rooms and meal functions. We also need to discuss dates."

As it turned out, this hotel didn't have the dates available either. But the Agile Manager gladly changed his meeting plans and rearranged airline schedules.

Why? Simple—because of a sales professional who made the difference by conducting an outstanding, customer-focused sales interview.

Postscript: The meeting went off without a hitch. And waiting for the Agile Manager to help kick off the meeting was a live St. Bernard. The hotel's salesperson had made arrangements with the dog's owner to have "Bernie" available for pictures with each member of the sales organization.

The old way of selling was very much product-focused. It went something like this:

1. Tell the customer what is new.
2. Explain a new product's features, functions, and benefits.
3. Compare these to what the customer now has.
4. Lead the customer to the "right" decision.

A Better Way: Focus on the Customer

There's a better way of selling. In it, customer-focused solutions—those geared specifically to your prospect's needs—are the ultimate objective.

The customer-focused selling approach:

1. Creates interest by talking to people about things they're interested in;

2. Uncovers needs, goals, priorities, and a personal win;

3. Crafts a customer-focused solution.

Customer-focused selling is the only way prospects can get the full value from the products or services they buy. It's also the only way you, the salesperson, can get "full value" for the time you expend to get the sale. And it's the only way to turn a one-time buyer into a dedicated customer.

Why? Consider a simple situation in which price is exactly equal to value.

Price $=$ **Value**

Is there a compelling reason for somebody to do business with you? No. Most people want to feel like they are getting more value for their money than they are paying.

Those using product-focused selling approaches understand this, too. But unfortunately, the way they increase value is by cutting the price! That creates the illusion of value.

Worse, the pressures of meeting sales quotas prompts sales-people to cut the price even more.

In this scenario, neither the customer, nor the salesperson, gets full value. Why not the customer? Because those buying on price alone may not stop long enough to consider whether the product or service is solving a problem most efficiently for them.

Customer-focused selling provides a far better way to increase value than to cut the cost. You identify a minimum of three value-added benefits to create a compelling reason for someone to do business with you. These value-added benefits go over and above meeting minimum specifications. They usually involve things like:

- Increasing customer satisfaction
- Improving productivity and efficiency
- Saving time
- Reducing costs
- Protecting previous investments
- Gaining a competitive edge and growing market share

When you are actually able to provide benefits of this type, you're providing real value that will often eliminate the need to discount price. Why? You're providing a customer *enablers* that positively impact business.

Understanding your strengths, and the value you provide, binds your relationship, builds your business, keeps the competition out, and positions you to leverage past success for future growth.

Interviewing: The Heart of the Sales Process

The heart of customer-focused selling is conducting an effective sales interview. Salespeople should know how to assemble various probing and questioning skills to learn the prospect's or customer's needs, wants, dreams, and goals. You can then present a *value-added solution* that best answers these requirements.

A value-added solution is the objective of a customer-focused sales interview. And "value" is from the prospect's perspective, not yours. The right questions determine what benefits your prospect considers "value added." This distinguishes you and your company from your competition.

Best Tip

Take the time to provide a customer-focused solution. It's the only way to turn a buyer into a dedicated customer.

A benefit for you is that having a system for conducting customer-focused interviews quickly establishes your personal credibility. This system saves time and helps you determine what is most important to your prospect.

Consider Organizational Dynamics

Because you may sell at multiple levels within an organization, you have to vary your approach according to the position. Why? Would you conduct an interview with the chief financial officer in the same way you would with the marketing manager? Probably not. They have different interests and different agendas.

The chart on the following page shows what these interests commonly are. Use it to craft questions and solutions that address these concerns directly.

USE THE F.I.N.D. INTERVIEW SYSTEM

In the heat of battle, some salespeople may forget to ask important questions. This means they have to call back later to get information. Speaking to a top manager, even by telephone, can take a lot of time and will delay the sales process if you're not prepared. That makes you appear disorganized.

To keep this from happening to you, use our simple customer-

What Interests Various Jobholders

President, Division V.P., General Manager
- Satisfying customers
- Growing profitably
- Increasing the company's value (stock price)
- Gaining a competitive advantage
- Improving productivity
- Finding and retaining good people

CFO, Treasurer, Finance Manager
- Improving return on investment
- Watching the "bottom line"
- Controlling costs
- Financing options
- Cash flow
- Budgets

CIO, CTO, V.P. for MIS, MIS Director
- Aligning MIS with corporate goals
- Satisfying customers (internal and external)
- Leveraging investment in MIS
- Industry trends
- Security and control
- Proving his/her value

V.P. for Sales, Sales Manager
- Crushing the sales quota
- Increasing sales rep productivity
- Improving customer satisfaction
- Enhancing profit margins
- Finding and developing good people
- Getting leads and finding other methods to grow the business

V.P. or Director of Manufacturing, Manager of Manufacturing
- Supporting business model
- Meeting deadlines
- Maintaining or improving quality
- Managing capital equipment efficiently
- Minimizing downtime
- Standardizing procedures

Contract/Procurement Manager, Purchasing Agent
- Getting the most value for the money
- Getting compliance with terms and conditions
- Competitive price and delivery
- Vendor relationships
- Proving his/her value

V.P. or Director of Marketing, Manager of Marketing
- Increasing market share
- Gaining competitive edge
- Increasing brand awareness
- Maximizing budget dollars
- Reducing time to market
- Protecting customer base

V.P. or Director of Operations, Manager of Operations
- Aligning operations with corporate goals
- Maximizing productivity
- Following procedures
- Meeting deadlines
- Smoothing operations
- Minimizing downtime

focused interviewing system, F.I.N.D. The F.I.N.D. System assists you in asking questions about the four critical areas required to structure a customer-focused solution. F.I.N.D. stands for:

FACTS. Gather background information on the customer's organization and situation, what products the company currently uses, how it now handles maintenance and support, who supplies services, and what it likes best and least with all of the above.

IMPORTANT ISSUES. Understand what important issues must be satisfied by current or new suppliers (increased sales, reduced costs, etc.). Having this all-important information will help you frame the general discussion to follow.

|Best *Tip*

Ask, 'In your opinion, why do your customers do business with you?' The answer can reveal benefits the prospect deems important.

NEEDS. Uncover problems with internal operations, areas the company's current approach does not address, and additional benefits the customer might be looking for.

DREAMS. Uncover both a business and personal win for the customer and expand his thinking beyond the immediate future. That helps him form a plan of action to reach his dreams.

Every F.I.N.D. interview has one main objective: Identify, rank, and explore the three key issues that your prospect is most interested in and determine her important business needs as well as personal dreams tied to business.

Once you have that information, you can frame your offering around these issues with a customer-focused presentation or proposal using the specific features offered by your solution (plus any additional services and support you provide).

1. Warm-up: Get the Facts

Confirm how much time you have, then begin the interview

by asking open-ended questions and probes about the general state of the industry. Then transition into a discussion about the customer's company.

This is the warm-up, and the time to gather facts. These questions are easy for the prospect to answer. If you have done some preliminary research about the company, you can quickly establish your credibility by asking the prospect to confirm information you have already gathered. Examples:

Sales Professional's Hot Tip #4

Questions Are the Answer. Probes and questions are critical in selling. The better you probe and ask customer-focused questions, the more successful you will become. Many of the sales greats believe their higher sales come from the quality of the questions they ask.

Probes are sentences that begin with action verbs like *give*, *describe, tell, talk*, and *explain*.

Probes can be used as conversation starters, to uncover a person's feelings and values, or to reveal general information. Probes ask your listener to provide you with background information and their feelings on a subject.

Questions are more direct than probes. They ask the listener for specific information on a subject. Questions can also identify customer wants, needs, dreams, goals, and a personal win.

Questions come in two forms: *open ended* and *closed ended*.

Open-ended questions are great for getting people to open up and converse with you freely. They ask your customers or prospects for specific information (the facts) and their opinions (their feelings). Open-ended questions begin with the words *what, where, why, when, how*, and *who*.

Closed-ended questions start with words like *do you, did they, would you, will she, can you*, etc. They ask for specific yes/no, this one/that one, or either/or types of answers.

Don't use closed-ended questions if you want to get your prospect to open up to you. Use them, however, if you are asking for a commitment to action, confirmation, or decision.

"I understand from your recent press release that the competition's price cutting has contributed to eroding margins industrywide. What area has been affected the most within your organization?"

"I read about your plans to open new offices next year. Which will come on line first?"

Try to go beyond cold facts to learn something about the prospect's feelings, opinions, and impressions.

One really thought-provoking question is: "In your opinion, why do your customers do business with your organization?"

B*est* T*ip*
Find out which three or four issues are of prime interest to your prospect—and what they mean, exactly, to the prospect.

The answer will usually contain value-added benefits, beyond low price, the company provides. Try it when you're selling to another business. The information may come in handy later if you get a price objection.

Also, it's a great way to show the person you are interviewing that you are interested in being in step or in synch with them. Later on, you can demonstrate your attentiveness by playing back the answer.

By the way, to help solicit quality responses, preface important questions with, "In your opinion . . ." It focuses people better.

2. Uncover the Important Issues

In the second part of the F.I.N.D. Interview System, you focus on exploring the issues that are most important to your prospect. (Refer again to the chart a few pages back.) Come into the interview armed with a list of likely candidates, like reduced costs, higher productivity, etc. And refer to the same issues you mentioned when prospecting. After all, you created interest with those issues and got the appointment.

Begin phase two by talking about these issues in a general

F.I.N.D. Interview System Preparation Worksheet

FACTS: To determine background information on what products and services prospects currently use, how they currently handle maintenance and support, who supplies services to them, what they like best and least.

QUESTIONS TO USE: Simple/general, fact finding, historical. "In your opinion, why do your customers do business with you?" "What are some of the greatest challenges you face this year?"

PURPOSE: To start conversations, learn about current operations.

IMPORTANT ISSUES: To understand what important issues must be satisfied by current or new suppliers, and to provide important information to frame the general discussion that will follow. List three important issues of interest to the prospect.

QUESTIONS TO USE: Fact finding, historical, situational, exploratory, investigative. "From our experience working with other people in your position, we've learned that the three issues they seem most interested in are: increasing customer satisfaction, improving productivity, and growing their businesses profitably. Are these the three most important issues you face? Which is most important? How do you measure them now?" "What are your goals for improvement?"

PURPOSE: Establish credibility and trust, understand prospect's views.

NEEDS: To uncover problems with internal systems, areas current suppliers do not address, and what additional benefits prospects are looking for in a new partner or supplier.

QUESTIONS TO USE: Fact finding, historical, situational, exploratory, investigative, hypothetical, agreement/closing. "What problems are keeping you awake at night?" "What needs to happen for you to reach your goals?"

PURPOSE: Identify problems, qualify, evaluate alternatives.

DREAMS: To uncover both a business and personal win for prospects, and to expand their thinking beyond the immediate future to help them formulate a plan of action to reach their dreams.

QUESTIONS TO USE: Situational, exploratory, investigative, hypothetical, agreement/closing. "If we are able to accomplish all you want, what will it mean to you on a personal level?"

PURPOSE: Identify their wins, shape their thinking, bind your relationship.

sense. Then ask a closed-ended question to see if your prospect agrees. ("Do you agree?")

If he does, probe to see which issues are most important, why, and what they mean to the business. For example, a general manager might select improving productivity as a top priority. Probe to see what makes that issue so important. You'll also want to know exactly what improving productivity means to that person.

Here's a probe you might ask of that general manager: "Please tell me why improving productivity is so important to you. What would the impact of that be?"

If the prospect doesn't agree with one or more items on your list, ask what issues should be on the list. Then, find out what makes them important to the business.

Either way, identify, rank, and explore the meaning of the top three or four key issues. Gather-

Best Tip

Find out who your competition for the business is and if they can offer the prospect anything that you can't.

ing this information becomes critical for your proposal or presentation, because you'll respond to these issues in the same order.

You will also use these issues to frame the remainder of your customer-focused interview. If return on investment is important, for example, explore (quantify) what the prospect considers excellent, average, and minimum ROI figures.

Ultimately, you'll wrap your solution around these important issues when you present a customer-focused solution. This will differentiate you from average salespeople. To your prospect you will look, act, and sound like a consultant, because that is exactly what you are!

3. Identify Prospects' Needs

The third stage of the F.I.N.D. Interview System zeros in on the specific benefits your prospects need. Once you have identified, ranked, and explored the important issues facing your prospect, ask open-ended questions to uncover problems with the present situation. Identify the benefits she desires. These will become opportunities for you.

Probe to determine if the prospect is evaluating other alternatives. Find out who the competition is, and ask if the competition is impressive in any way. Determine the prospect's timetable for taking action, assuming she found the perfect solution. Then qualify this person's actual buying authority. Ask if anyone else will be involved in making the final decision.

Sample questions:

"If you could change the present operation, what would you do first to address the problem?"

"Which alternative approach has impressed you the most?"

"Who else in the company will you consult with in reaching your final decision?"

Use hypothetical questions to overcome the prospect's hesitation or resistance. This will help to expand the scope of her thinking and perhaps even reframe it (more on this when we get to objections). Then ask closed-ended questions that confirm you have identified key needs. Be certain your prospect agrees.

Examples:

"I understand. Just suppose it was a top priority. What would you do first?"

"So if I understand correctly, you'd drop that procedure before the quarter ended if you could?"

Self-Check

Ask yourself this question immediately after the customer-focused interview to determine how effective you were:

Who did most of the talking?

If the answer is your prospect—congratulations.

4. Explore Dreams

Even the owner of the candy store on the corner dreams about the day the business will expand from one shop to two. Then from two shops to three, to five, and more. Think about your dreams: Where you are today? Where do you want to be next year? Where do you want to be in three years?

Best Tip

Helping prospects reach their dreams is a powerful lever that can motivate them to do business with you.

Your prospects also have dreams about their businesses and their careers. If they own the business, they may want to expand to other cities, or they might wish they had more free time to be with their families, or to go boating or fishing.

If they don't own the business, they may dream about their next big bonus, getting promoted, having fewer hassles or problems, or whatever else is important to them.

Uncovering the prospect's dreams is critical in the customer-focused interview. If you can find a dream, you can identify a personal win. When you do, you can then bring together a customer-focused solution that addresses business issues and that win.

Your solution will then help the prospect fulfill his dreams. This may be the most compelling reason to do business with you and your company.

Example:

"What would it mean to you personally to make these goals a reality?"

When to Ask the "Dream" Question. When asking about personal dreams, make sure your prospect is the only one from the organization present. That way he can speak freely.

But wait until you feel you've established credibility and trust. Your gut will tell you when you've achieved this position.

Some people will provide the information without being asked. You can often ask the question during the first meeting. And sometimes it takes several encounters with a prospect before the time is right. It's OK to conduct a solid F.I.N.D. interview and still get to the personal win at another time.

Tie It All Together

Once you have confirmed the *F*acts, identified *I*mportant *I*ssues, uncovered *N*eeds, and explored your prospect's *D*reams, what do you do next?

Some salespeople may want to present a solution right away. Though there are times this may be appropriate, we don't recommend it.

Generally, the customer-focused sale requires you to go back to your office and study the information you've just uncovered. You need to analyze which of your products, solutions and support services will provide the specific benefits the prospect is looking for. Only then will you be ready to present the customer-focused solution that best fits your prospect's issues, needs, and dreams.

Make an appointment for another day to present your findings. Understand, however, that prospects will usually want you to provide some information during the initial interview about what you're thinking. After all, they have just invested their time and want you to solve the puzzle.

Make only general recommendations at this point. It's too early to get specific. First you need to study the alternatives and prepare a well thought-out proposal, presentation, or demonstration.

Multiple Decision Makers. If others are involved in the decision, ask your prospect to introduce you to any other people you need to speak with. Interview each of the decision makers, individually if possible. You may need to collect more specific information, details, or other perspectives.

This is especially true for buying committees. Don't propose your solution until you've spoken with all the people you need to. It takes more time, but it helps you avoid surprises. Also, it's much more professional.

The Agile Sales Manager, feet on his desk, recalled many interesting answers he had received to the question regarding the personal win or dream. Some of these answers included earning the respect of peers, getting a promotion or bonus, keeping their current position as opposed to being terminated, and, quite often, "getting a life"—free time!

The one common trait among all the hundreds of times the Agile Manager had asked the dream question was how people really opened up once he had established credibility and trust. As a result, he was in a much better position to help prospective customers get what they wanted.

He remembered in particular calling on the president of a small foundry.

The Agile Manager asked, "If it were three months from now, and our organizations worked together to help you realize the business objectives that you just laid out, what satisfaction would that give you on a personal basis?"

The president rose out of his conference room chair. "You'll have to follow me into the men's room. There is something there I'd like to show you."

The Agile Manager had found himself in some strange positions during his career, but this one had the potential to beat all.

Once inside the men's room, the president said, "One of the big benefits to me personally would be if I could come in here for just five minutes and not be interrupted." With that, he kicked open the door to one of the stalls to reveal a bright red telephone.

"If this project works," he said, "I'll be able to rip that thing down. Imagine the satisfaction that would give me!"

As the Agile Manager likes to tell his salespeople, he secured the business even though the solution he provided was neither the least expensive nor the most rich with features. And, he adds, "I'm pretty certain that the president didn't invite any of the competing salespeople into the men's room!"

The Agile Manager's Checklist

✔ Create value by adding benefits, not by cutting the price.

✔ Keep in mind that "value" and "benefit" must be judged from the buyer's perspective, not yours.

✔ Use the F.I.N.D. interview system to uncover facts, important issues, needs, and dreams.

✔ After the sales interview, go back to the office and put together a solution tailored precisely to the prospect's needs.

Chapter Five

Plan and Deliver
An Outstanding Proposal

When the Agile Sales Manager first joined his organization, he learned about the product line by attending as many demonstrations as possible. All of them had much happier endings than the first one he observed.

He arrived at a branch-office demonstration room about ninety minutes prior to a 2:00 P.M. demonstration. There he found someone in the midst of cleaning up a mess that had been left by the last user of the room.

"Hi, I'm Bob Smith," said the man. He was the salesperson the Agile Manager would observe.

The Agile Manager shook his hand and said, "You have quite a mess here. Let me help you out. Who are you doing a demonstration for today?"

"The biggest bank in the region," replied Bob. "We'll have four people in. One of them is the decision maker. I haven't been able to talk to him before this."

"What are they really interested in? What's their biggest need?" asked the Agile Manager.

"I really don't know. The technical capabilities seemed of great interest to the information-systems guys. They were really excited about seeing our newest bells and whistles. I figure we'll knock their socks off with the speed we can demonstrate."

"And the benefit to their business of that speed?"

"Can't say for sure," said Bob.

The Agile Manager was shocked that he had no clear understanding of the prospect's needs and objectives. Bob was going to talk a lot about product features and functions hoping, along the way, to identify benefits to the prospect.

This, the Agile Manager knew, was not a customer-focused approach, and the prospect represented one of the largest financial institutions in the country.

When they finished cleaning up, Bob said, "I've got a few things to do. I'll be back at 1:45 to meet with one of our technical support people. She'll be working the equipment while I talk."

The Agile Manager said nothing as Bob left. He was surprised that he and the technical support person would meet for only fifteen minutes. Oh well, he thought, they must have spent a few hours together already.

But when they reconvened at 1:45, it was clear the two had never met. Bob rushed through the instructions, and the Agile Manager could see that the technician wasn't sure what to do, or when. He found himself secretly wishing that the prospect would miss the demo due to a last-minute scheduling change.

But just as he finished that thought, four people from the financial institution walked through the door eager to get things started.

Half an hour into the presentation—despite its sloppiness—the senior member of the group said, "You know, that's just the type of capability that could really handle some of our biggest problems."

Bob was smart enough to recognize a buying signal. He said, "I'm happy that you feel that way. Would you like to review the preliminary agreement I drafted and discuss implementation?"

The group considered the question for a few moments, until the technician broke the silence by saying, "I haven't even shown you half the capabilities of the system. Why don't I show you the rest?"

The buying group seemed happy to see more, but Bob scowled at the technician.

He tried no fewer than eight more times to reintroduce the point and get commitment. The more he pushed, the more he put off those in the group, especially the senior executive. Finally, he told Bob, "I think we've been pushed hard enough for one day. You must be really desperate for an order."

Bob said, "No, please don't go. I'm sorry . . ." But everyone had already put on their coats and headed out the door.

After they'd gone, Bob lit into the technician. "You really blew it for us. I had them on the hook until you jumped in about wanting to show them more!"

"Now, now," said the Agile Manager. He figured he'd try to salvage the situation by doing a little coaching. "That wasn't a smart move, to be sure. But I think if you'd done a little more preparation . . ."

Have you ever made what you thought was an excellent presentation or proposal, but which did not result in an order? What happened? Most likely, you didn't properly prepare to address the prospect's real needs.

Never forget: The prospect decides whether a presentation is excellent or not. What you think is immaterial.

For a demonstration to be really effective, it must do more than make the sales team feel good. It must cause the prospect to take positive action. A value-added solution, remember, distinguishes you from the competition. If you gather the right information, you will be able to provide answers to the key issues the prospect feels are important.

Recommending the best solution is one of the most important skills in customer-focused selling. You need to prepare in advance and think about your presentation or proposal carefully. And you'll want to maintain the consultative sales approach you've used thus far.

Solve Problems, Provide Benefits

One thing to keep in mind as you move through the sales process: Prospects are not interested in features. They are interested in the value (benefits) of these features. It is critically important that you keep this in mind when you make a customer-focused demonstration or presentation. If you don't, you'll be reciting technical specifications, and your presentation soon becomes product-focused.

People don't want to hear a "talking brochure," they want to learn how you can solve a problem, satisfy a need, and help them achieve their goals.

When you describe features, functions, and benefits:

- Keep it simple.
- Keep it relevant.
- Keep it interesting.
- Relate everything to the prospect's interests, needs, priorities, and dreams.

Structure your proposal or presentation as follows:

I. The prospect's major issues, needs, goals, and priorities.

Sales Professional's Hot Tip #5

Use Your Selling Time Wisely

1. Use the hours between 8:00 A.M. and 5:00 P.M. to speak with prospects and customers.

2. Whenever possible, write proposals, letters, quotations, etc., during the hours you can't speak with prospects (early morning, evenings, weekends).

3. Fill out your prospect lists, sales reports, and forecasts during the times you can't speak with prospects.

4. Offload non-selling activities to anyone you can find who will do them for you.

5. Be more proactive. Let people know when you're available to meet and give them options.

II. Your approach to providing a solution

III. The features and functions of your approach.

IV. How the benefits of your approach satisfy the prospect's interests, needs, priorities, and dreams.

V. Incremental benefits from additional features that are included with your approach.

Checklist for Effective Presentations

Sales demonstrations and presentations vary a great deal, depending on the audience. Some will be casual pitches to a single prospect. Others will be much more formal and for a group.

Most situations will allow you enough time to prepare properly. But sometimes you have to do a presentation before you get the chance to determine needs, important issues, goals, and priorities.

It's usually a poor use of both the prospect's time and yours to present without some level of understanding. It won't be as meaningful. Therefore, begin by asking questions to get the audience involved and to share vital information.

Best Tip

Plan and structure your presentation with one goal in mind: causing the prospect to take positive action.

For example, "For this investment of time to be most beneficial to you, I'd like to get your opinions on some things that will allow me to be specific in meeting your needs, issues, goals, and priorities." Then, use the F.I.N.D. Interview System to gather information.

Serious prospects respect the logic behind this approach. It allows you to focus on aspects of your solution that are most relevant to the prospect's unique situation.

Whether making a formal or informal presentation, to a group or to an individual, keep these ten things in mind.

1. Know your prospect's important issues, needs, goals and priorities, and dreams by conducting a customer-focused interview.

2. Plan, with all the players on your sales team, who'll be involved. Share the information you have and clearly define each participant's role.

3. Know which of your products and services will help solve the prospect's problems.

4. Present a complete solution, not just a small portion.

5. Customize your presentation to your prospect.

6. Use literature and visual aids when appropriate—but don't start by passing out brochures! You want the prospect to focus on you. Pass out brochures later.

7. Speak the prospect's language by tying your ideas and solutions to his specific situation.

8. Keep the prospect involved during the entire presentation. Ask questions, and look her in the eye. *Listen* to the answers.

9. Justify the cost of your solution by providing return on investment (ROI) calculations and evidence to back up any claims.

10. Verify that the prospect understands your approach and accepts it as viable. Ask confirming questions along the way, such as "Do you see how that function solves your problem?" And, "Does that address your needs?"

Adjust Your Presentation for the Person

It's important to adjust your demonstrations and sales presentations to match the buying style of your prospect. A serious mistake that many salespeople make is to use the identical format for all prospects.

Remember: For a demonstration or sales presentation to be successful, the prospect must take positive action. For that to happen, you need to shape the presentation around the prospect's personality type. Pay attention to the prospect from your very first contact—and even before-

| Best Tip

Present a complete solution customized precisely to the needs of your prospect.

hand by asking questions of others who know the individual. When you do, you gain insight into her personality in the situation or environment you'll meet her.

We've found that there are four main behavior styles.* Observing and listening to a prospect will aid you in determining if the person:

- Likes to dominate and control,
- Is outgoing and friendly,
- Focuses on a systematic approach and is security minded,
- Is careful and analytical.

Dominance Style

Those of this style try to dominate and control. Such a person:

- Is fast-paced and assertive
- Shows decisiveness
- Is demanding and direct
- Does more "telling" than "asking"

When the prospect is dominating and controlling:

1. Stick to business. Don't get too personal.

2. Be clear, specific, brief, and to the point.

3. Use a paper-based executive summary in bullet-point form. Put the most important point first. Keep the list to three or four items if possible.

4. Come prepared with a well-organized package. Make it easy for this sometimes-impatient person to find things by labeling them well. Put documents concerning the prospect's important issues and how you'd address them up front.

5. Have support materials ready, but don't go into details unless you're asked.

---

*The ideas that follow are adapted from Carlson Learning Company's DiSC® Model and Personal Profile System®. We strongly endorse both.(DiSC® and Personal Profile System® are registered trademarks of Carlson Learning Company.)

6. Present your case logically.

7. Tie up all loose ends.

8. Provide facts and figures about the effectiveness of options.

9. Provide alternatives and options that allow the individual to make his own decision. Example: "To meet your needs, either of these two approaches would work. You can decide which and then control the implementation."

10. Persuade by referring constantly to the objectives and results the prospect is looking for.

Power words to use with dominating, controlling people:			
Bottom line	Growth	Dominate	Attain
Control	Attack	Eliminate	Earn
Capitalize	Productivity	Results	Impact
Achieve	Decisive	Productive	
Competitive advantage			

Influential Style

Those of this style are friendly and outgoing. Such a person:

- Is spontaneous
- Enjoys social conversation
- Is enthusiastic and animated
- Shows more interest in people than things

When the prospect is friendly and outgoing:

1. Allow time for socializing.

2. Be informal, friendly, and warm.

3. Talk about people and their goals first.

4. Ask for their opinions again.

5. Put the details in writing, but don't dwell on them.

6. Provide ideas for implementing your proposal.

7. Offer testimonials from prominent people and companies.

8. Offer special incentives.

9. Provide alternatives that feature teamwork.

Power words to use with friendly, outgoing people			
People	Vision	Image	Team
Inspire	Recognition	Motivate	Looking good
Influence	Results	Achieve	Rally
Partner	Empower	Fantastic	Communicate

10. Persuade them by mentioning their dreams.

Steadiness Style

Those of this style are systematic and security-minded. Such a person:

- Likes process-related questions
- Allows you plenty of time
- Is often indirect
- Is friendly but reserved

When the prospect is systematic and security-minded:

1. Begin slowly. Break the ice with a personal comment.
2. Present your proposal softly and in a nonthreatening way.
3. Review the prospect's goals and objectives.
4. Present your solution in a step-by-step approach.
5. Put the details in writing, but don't dwell on them.
6. Offer assurances that minimize risks.
7. Include the procedures for implementation and for handling problem areas.

Power words to use with systematic, security-minded people:			
Secure	Stable	Process	Measurements
Procedures	Cooperate	Back-up plan	Teamwork
Responsive	Participate	First, second, third	
System	Safe	Plan for problem solving	
Plan for problem resolution		Plan for problem anticipation	

8. Get the prospect's agreement on critical issues—especially the need for "orderly" change.

9. Justify your ideas with hard facts.

10. Persuade by summarizing the important benefits of your proposed solutions.

Conscientiousness Style

Those of this style tend to be careful and analytical. This person:

- Is interested in details
- Takes a great deal of time to verify the facts
- Expresses a cautious attitude that stresses quality and reliability
- Is more interested in logic than emotion

When the prospect is careful and analytical:

1. Prepare carefully in advance. Have a well-organized package.

2. Be straightforward and direct. Don't get too personal.

3. Include support materials at all critical points.

4. Take your time. Expect lots of questions and a longer decision-making process.

5. Provide both the pros and cons of your recommendations.

6. Offer multiple choices and provide the pluses and minuses of each.

7. Have a schedule for implementing the solution.

8. Allow time for the prospect to digest and verify your data. Avoid special offers good for a limited time only.

9. Prove your case with solid, tangible evidence.

10. Persuade prospects by comparing the important benefits of your proposition to those of your competition.

Power words to use with careful, analytical people			
Analyze	Quality	Sensible	Planning
Best available	Tested	Cautious	Think
Logical	Detailed	Critical	Proven
Research	Reengineered		

Sales Professional's Hot Tip #6

Have Lunch with Customers/Prospects. Successful sales-people have lunch with customers and prospects whenever they can. It pays rich dividends. (And don't expect your company to pay for all your business entertainment.) Some thoughts:

- Most salespeople do not entertain their customers and prospects enough.
- Customers may feel a slight obligation to you when you buy lunch. Plus, you get to talk to prospects outside of the noise and confusion of the office.
- Lunches are great for building lasting personal relationships.
- Don't discuss business until your customer/prospect does.

Sell to Committees

The same principles apply when you demonstrate or present to committees as when you deal with individuals. It is especially important to remember not to turn a committee sales demonstration into a lecture. It's critical to involve actively all the members of the committee.

To accomplish this, be sure you conduct a customer-focused sales interview with *each* member of the committee before you make a presentation. While this means you have to do a lot more work, it's the only way you can include "something for everyone."

On the next page you'll find an example of an "Issues Cluster Matrix." It can help you organize and plan for the most important issues of different committee members.

On the matrix, you chart the number of times people on the buying committee bring up specific issues. That helps you determine which issues are of the greatest importance.

The Issues Cluster Matrix allows for something else of critical importance—weighing each committee member's votes according to his or her power in the organization.

In this example, the CEO receives 2 votes per issue mentioned, the director and department manager I receive 1 vote, and department manager II receives half a vote. You can play around with the weighting scheme based on your subjective assessment of the committee's power structure.

Important issues for this committee would be prioritized and addressed in this order:

1. Increased customer satisfaction (4.5 votes)
2. Increased employee productivity (3.5 votes)
3. Single vendor responsibility (3 votes)
4. Security and control (2.5 votes)
5. Complete problem management (1.5 votes)

Issues Cluster Matrix				
Important Issues	**Key Players**			
	CEO	Director	Department Manager 1	Department Manager 2
Increased Customer Satisfaction	2	1	1	.5
Increased Employee Productivity	2		1	.5
Single Vendor Responsibility	2	1		
Complete Problem Management			1	.5
Security and Control		1	1	.5

> ## *Sales Professional's Hot Tip #7*
> **Don't Waste Time Making Poor Calls**
>   1. Prepare for each call in advance, and have an objective. Rate the success of each call.
>   2. Qualify prospects as early as possible. The second best answer you receive can be "no."
>   3. Know when to walk away.

When Presenting to a Committee

Before you begin your demonstration or sales presentation, thank the people who spent time with you. Review your list of the issues that are important to them. Check to see if anything has changed. There may be additions, corrections, deletions, changed priorities, etc.

Follow this with a general statement on how your solution will address these important issues.

During the presentation, involve the participants. As you address each issue, look at the committee members who are concerned with it. Remind them that this was one of their concerns, and try to get their agreement that your solution takes care of the issue.

Pause often to ensure everyone understands you. Encourage people to ask questions, and secure their agreement at each critical point. Taking "temperature readings" like these makes closing much easier.

Address the issues of the decision maker and the domineering types first. Then address the issues brought up by the friendly and outgoing, the security-minded, and the analytical committee members, in that order.

Note: A committee will often have a "fox." Be vigilant; the fox may be dressed in sheep's clothing. The fox may not say much, but he will influence the committee's decision.

The fox may be a natural devil's advocate, a quiet but influential person, or someone appointed to poke holes in your arguments.

The fox usually won't undermine you while you're presenting. He'll do that later. That's why it's a good practice to ask questions to flush out hidden feelings and then address them. "I'd like to be sure everyone agrees with our approach in that area before I move on. What concerns do you have Mr. Fox?"

Watch for Buying Signals

When you become proficient at identifying interests, needs, priorities, and dreams, and you convert this knowledge into a good customer-focused demonstration or sales presentation, you can expect to see buying signals from your prospect. When you see a buying signal, finish what you are doing and close the sale.

> **Best Tip**
>
> Encourage questions, and secure agreement with your views and ideas at critical points in the presentation.

Prospects can signal they are ready to buy in many ways. They can signal "Okay, I'm sold," with body language, the questions they ask, and their actions. Be observant and recognize buying signals whenever they occur.

Some of the more distinctive buying signals are when the prospect:

- Reads your proposal's terms and conditions carefully.
- Examines information or documentation carefully.
- Becomes relaxed, friendly, and demonstrates open body language.
- Begins nodding up and down quickly at what you say.
- Begins asking you for price concessions or special services.
- Brings in an associate to review your documentation.
- Asks you to repeat answers to questions about terms, products, programs, and services.

Try a Trial Close

Some salespeople get so caught up in the presentation that they miss or—worse—ignore the prospect's buying signals. That's a shame. How many times have you heard about a rep who has "talked himself out of the sale"?

Whenever you get a buying signal from a prospect, follow up immediately with a trial close. Ask a closed-ended question like, "Are you ready to move forward today?" Other possibilities:

"Should we review the paperwork to begin implementation?"

"Since the benefits are all here in our recommendation, when can we expect your purchase order?"

Questions like these save you time, either because you'll gain a quick agreement, or because you'll uncover a concern, problem, or objection that you can deal with.

Be sure you communicate your plans for dealing with buying signals with the other members of your team. And after asking a trial closing question, let the person answer fully before you start talking again.

The Agile Manager's Checklist

✔ Continue to use a consultative sales approach when presenting a proposal. Stress benefits, not features.
✔ Best advice when presenting: Keep it simple, relevant, and interesting.
✔ Become aware of the four behavior styles: Dominance, Influential, Steadiness, and Conscientious. Adjust your presentation to the style.
✔ Be on the alert for buying signals. If you get one, try a trial close.

Chapter Six

Handle Objections

It was the last two weeks of the fiscal year. Les, who covered one of the more rural territories, was briefing the Agile Sales Manager about an upcoming sales call.

"And at four o'clock we'll stop at the Jones farm to pick up the contract for the order that I forecasted last month," said Les. He smiled and continued, "With that order I'll qualify for the incentive trip to Hawaii."

"That's great," said the Agile Manager. "I bet your wife is pretty excited about that."

"Well as a matter a fact," beamed Les, "she went to the mall just last night and bought a new suitcase and several outfits."

The Agile Manager and Les were greeted later that day at the farm by two brothers, both tall enough to be professional basketball players. On the way in to meet their eighty-year-old father, one of the brothers explained how badly they had wanted to act months ago on the decision to buy Les's solution to their problem.

"Dad is extremely frugal," said one of them, "and very deliberate when it comes to money." Although the sons played a big role in the success of the family's egg business, Dad ruled with a tight fist and made all final decisions.

Upon entering the office, the Agile Manager noticed an antique desk with a marble-based pen-and-pencil set. The only other thing on the desk was a pile of papers. Being skilled at reading upside down, the Agile Manager noted that it was their contract.

As they were seated, the old man behind the desk said, "Well Les, I'm glad to see you again. Young fellow, it certainly is nice to meet you," he said nodding to the Agile Manager. "The boys have convinced me that going with your organization is the right decision. Of course I also received the blessing of our banker, accountant, and attorney."

Taking the pen from the desk set, he said, "The papers appear to be in order. There is no reason why we can't get started on this right now." Everyone was smiling, especially the two sons. The Agile Manager noticed that they appeared to be even more excited than Les about the order.

Just as the pen was about to touch the paper, the old man looked at Les and raised a simple, innocent objection in the form of a question. "This product will work with that new conveyor line we're thinking about, won't it?"

It was so harmless and inconsequential that a simple "yes," "no," or "maybe" would have sufficed.

But Les was suddenly struck down with that terrible affliction that even the most experienced salespeople suffer from occasionally: *Let-me-tell-you-all-that-I-knowitis.* He gave a lengthy, completely unnecessary explanation.

Les rambled on for three or four minutes and would have continued, except that the father's head slowly drooped down and came to rest upon the antique desk.

The Agile Manager feared the worst—that Dad had died. But he was relieved when he heard the sound of deep snores. Les stopped talking and the two brothers stared coldly at him. The Agile Manager reached down to pick up the pen; it had fallen on the floor and was resting against the old man's black-wing tip shoe. He managed to make just enough noise to wake him up.

"Well boys," he said, "with the information that Les was kind enough to provide, we're going to have to think this thing over some more and probably consult with our outside advisors. Les, I suggest that you call us in about thirty days. No, don't do that. I just remembered—the wife and I will be taking off for a six-week vacation middle of next month. You better make that just after Thanksgiving."

Considering the fiscal year ended September 30, and he needed this sale to get the trip to Hawaii, Les did his best to undo the damage he had done. Nothing worked.

Outside his father's office, son number one, towering over Les by a good foot, said, "I have a pretty good idea why your parents decided to give you the name that they did." The Agile Manager intervened and apologized for the debacle.

Eventually, Les did get the contract signed. Unfortunately, his wife never got to use the items purchased, for there was no trip to Hawaii. Not only did Les not qualify for the incentive reward, but the new fiscal year's commission plan resulted in his receiving only two-thirds of the money he would have received if he had only responded to a simple question with a direct answer.

Stalls, seeming indifference, and objections are normal in the sales process. There are ways to deal with all of them.

Customer-Focused Selling Wards Off Objections

One of the best ways to handle objections is to follow the customer-focused selling approach. When you do, you learn the issues, needs, goals, priorities, and personal win for your prospects. That's a great way to build a foundation of credibility and trust. This alone results in fewer objections. More important, the objections you get will usually be real concerns and not smoke screens.

Best Tip
Earn the trust of your prospects. That eliminates many objections and makes those you face easier to handle.

Nevertheless, every salesperson needs to be ready for an objection at any time.

Objections can be very different. Often, a salesperson may confuse a simple question with an objection. Or he may think a product shortcoming or request for special terms is a deal breaker. The better a salesperson handles these situations, the higher his sales will be.

Answer Simple Questions Directly

The first step in dealing with an objection is to determine whether it is a simple question, or if it is a real objection.

Whenever your prospect asks you a simple question, answer it. Simple questions require direct answers. Don't overstate or explain more than is required.

Use your judgment and common sense to determine if it's a simple or trick question. Simple questions are honest requests for information you haven't discussed yet, or clarification on something your prospect doesn't understand. After you respond, let the prospect decide if you've answered the question.

Sales Professional's Hot Tip #8			
Know the Value of Your Time			Your cost for wasting one hour per day per year
If you expect to earn	Each hour is worth	Each minute is worth	
$40,000	$20.00	$.33	$5,000
$50,000	$25.00	$.42	$6,250
$75,000	$37.50	$.63	$9,375
$85,000	$42.50	$.71	$10,625
$100,000	$50.00	$.83	$12,500
$150,000	$75.00	$1.25	$18,750
$175,000	$87.50	$1.46	$21,875
$200,000	$100.00	$1.67	$25,000
$225,000	$112.50	$1.88	$28,125
$250,000	$125.00	$2.08	$31,250

Remember: Place a value on your time. No one else will.

At times, you'll encounter trick questions. Trick questions may sound innocent, but they carry a hidden meaning or agenda. Again, use your judgment and common sense to decide if the question is a trick question.

For example, a prospect might ask:

"Is it a big deal if we want to get updates to any of this printed material?"

"No problem. We do it all the time," replies the salesperson.

"Well, since it's no problem, we'd expect there's no charge!"

If you think you're being asked a trick question, answer it with a question. This will usually force your prospect into giving you the real meaning of the question or the issue behind the question.

> **Best Tip**
>
> Answer a simple question simply. Let your prospect decide if you've answered it adequately.

In the example above, for instance, answer with something like, "Normally not, but what do you mean by big deal?" Or simply, "Why do you ask?" This may even uncover a bad prior experience with a current supplier.

Open the Prospect's Mind

Overcoming real objections requires opening up a prospect's mind just enough so the salesperson can "continue to sell."

Objections can be either hard (tangible) or soft (intangible).

Soft objections ("I'm happy with my present supplier") are really stalls on the prospect's part. They are another way of the prospect saying, "I'm not interested," or "I don't trust you yet."

Hard objections ("Our present supplier has a much better warranty") are usually the result of a product or service deficiency, price discrepancy, or a competitor's advantage.

Both types of objections are normal in the selling process. Soft objections can be more difficult to deal with sometimes, because they are disguised by a prospect who may be trying to avoid a confrontation.

You overcome objections regarding hard product or service deficiencies by opening the prospect's mind to see another point of view. Whatever the type of objection, you need a system to deal with them.

Six Steps to Overcoming Objections

The following is a simple system you can use to overcome most objections. By following this system, you will be able to:

- Identify and deal with the correct objection (a real problem)
- Avoid confrontations
- Reduce tension
- Build credibility and trust
- Create a favorable emotional climate
- Open closed minds to see things in a different light.

1. **LISTEN** to the entire objection. What is it about? What are the issues? Are they valid? What is the prospect saying? What is not being said? Are emotions high or low?

2. **ANALYZE** the type of objection and your response. Is the objection hard or soft? Valid or invalid? Easy or difficult to answer? What has caused the objection?

3. **SUPPORT** the prospect's right to object. Don't support the objection itself. The prospect is entitled to an opinion. To reduce tension, recognize that right. Acknowledge you understand his concern.

Don't complicate the objection. Avoid an immediate rebuttal or challenge. Buy yourself some extra time by making a supporting statement. For example, "I can appreciate how important this decision is to the business." Avoid using words like "but" or "however" after you make a supporting statement. Just pause for a few seconds instead.

Best Tip

Overcome objections by opening the prospect's mind enough to see another point of view.

4. CLARIFY the specifics and their importance. Gather additional information. Use open-ended questions and probes to identify issues. Is there a misunderstanding? What makes any perceived deficiencies important to the project? Are all issues on the table?

After the prospect provides additional information, you'll be better able to respond to the objection.

5. RESPOND with a simple explanation or a "reframe" dialogue (more on that in a moment). Offer proof, clarify, or explain. Update incorrect data. Open the prospect's mind to larger issues. Change the prospect's perspective by reviewing the goals

---

Know the Two Major Types of Objections

Hard Objections. Easy to identify, difficult to deal with because they usually involve tangible issues.

- High price
- Product/service failure
- Availability
- Disadvantage in the total solution offered
- Product disadvantage
- No budget
- No authority
- Bad prior experience with your company

Soft Objections. Tricky to identify and deal with because they usually involve intangible issues.

- Loyalty to a competitor
- Prospect is too busy
- Other priorities/not interested
- No immediate need
- Prospect takes a wait-and-see attitude (stall)
- Lack of credibility and trust in you or your company
- Doubts your products are necessary for success

and priorities you uncovered in the F.I.N.D. Interview.

6. VERIFY that you have dealt with the objection success-fully. If not, go back to step three and try again. Is the prospect satisfied with your response? Have you overcome the objection? Does the prospect agree?

Recently, the Agile Sales Manager observed this conversation between one of his salespeople, Mary and her prospect, Pat. He admired the way Mary overcame a key objection from Pat and set up a neat pathway to a close.

"Mary, I like your proposal but we don't want to be the first ones to install the system in our area."

"Pat, I understand how important this decision is." Mary paused for a moment, then continued. "What concerns do you have about the installation?"

Avoid rebutting an objection immediately. First offer a supportive statement.

"Well," Pat replied, "you said there was no place nearby that I could go to see it up and running. How do I know it's not filled with 'bugs' "?

"I apologize for not being clear earlier, Pat," Mary said sincerely. "We have customer installations all over the tri-state area—just not in this county. If you're willing to take a drive, we could visit a few."

"That'd be terrific," said Pat enthusiastically.

"If you were comfortable with the level of satisfaction most of the customers have, would you be ready to proceed with the order?"

"I sure would," said Pat. "Could we schedule visits next week?"

Reframe Objections to Open Minds

Reframing is one of the most powerful tools at your disposal to overcome objections. The following true example (the company name has been changed) illustrates the principles of reframing beautifully.

The Agile Sales Manager was speaking with Sarah, the senior account manager heading up the major-account sales team. She was explaining how her team was one of two finalists for a multimillion-dollar order with the Giftware Sales Company.

The opportunity involved replacing one thousand order-processing systems used by the company's distributors around the U.S. The current system was causing severe service problems, resulting in late deliveries and unrest among the distributors and other customers.

Giftware products are sold by a direct sales force at small house parties or local office functions. It's known for high-quality products, sold through a customer-oriented sales force. Because of this unique approach, it is able to command a premium price compared to less-expensive, imitation products. Any interruption in superb customer service hurts its image.

"We really have a wonderful opportunity," exclaimed Sarah. "Giftware has evaluated our system, and we meet all of its criteria. We also have the advantage of having a field-service organization. Our reputation in that regard is excellent, and service capability after the sale is a major criterion."

"Who is the other finalist?" asked the Agile Manager.

"That's the surprise in this deal," said Sarah. "The other finalist is a much smaller company that does not even have a field-service organization. They do, however, have a lower price, and that's a concern."

"How much lower?" asked the Agile Manager.

"As best as we can tell, 30 percent lower," Sarah replied. "And that's for the same configuration we're proposing."

The Agile Manager thought for a moment and then said, "It may appear to be the same, but it's not the same. Remember, we have our field-service organization. Hold your price. When is our meeting with Giftware?"

"A week from Friday," said Sarah.

Two days later, the Agile Manager's beeper went off while driving to the office. It was the senior account manager, Sarah.

"You won't believe what happened!" she said.

"What?" asked the Agile Manager.

"Giftware called our v.p. of field engineering, José Aguillar, and said it decided to buy the other company's system."

The Agile Manager replied, "I thought they weren't making a final decision until after our meeting on Friday."

"That's what we thought," said Sarah. "But they called to ask José if he would write a service agreement to maintain the other company's system!"

"What did he say?"

"He said he would. That was our major point of differentiation, you know. I called José and asked why he would do something like that. He said he made a 'business decision.' "

I'll give him a "business decision," thought the Agile Manager. Then he said, "Meet me at 10 A.M. We need to map out a plan to 'reframe' Giftware's thinking."

Later that morning at the planning session, the sales team discussed Friday's meeting with Giftware.

"Let's show them our new system," suggested one member of the team.

"That's not available yet. What's the point?" said another.

"Maybe we can stall the decision and buy ourselves some time," said another.

The Agile Manager said, "Tell me again: How did we hear they called our v.p. of service?"

"Giftware called and told us," said someone. "They asked if we could match the other company's price."

"So they haven't quite made a final decision. Good," said the Agile Manager.

Sarah jumped in and said, "They say both systems are essentially the same and since our service people would be handling maintenance, we need to think about lowering our price."

The Agile Manager said, "So they think both offerings are the same. I guess if any of us thought that way, we'd ask for a lower price, too."

"But they aren't the same system," said Sarah. "Our system is constructed to much higher specifications. We have pre-sales and post-sales support, the other guy doesn't. And we have a top-quality image and reputation."

"So we offer greater value than the competition?" asked the Agile Manager.

"Yes," said several people at once.

"But they don't see it, do they?" asked the Agile Manager. A few people murmured "no." He continued: "We need to open their minds—we need to reframe their thinking so they realize why we are different and why we are worth the higher price."

Reframing helps prospects expand their mindsets. People sometimes stand so close to something that they see only a small part of it. If you help them back up a few steps, they might see things from a different frame of reference or in a new light. Done well, reframing helps prospects see the "bigger picture."

Best Tip

Always verify that you've answered an objection to the prospect's satisfaction.

You always have an opportunity to open prospects' minds to broader issues, new ideas, and different solutions. This is what reframing is all about. The key is to reframe the prospect's thinking without starting an argument or making any challenging statements.

Two of the more advanced objection-handling techniques are the Analogy Reframe and the "Big Picture" Reframe.

The Analogy Reframe

When salespeople encounter a lack of interest from prospects, or when they say the problem is of low priority, the Analogy Reframe can be very effective.

This type of objection usually occurs when a prospect can't quite grasp the value of your solution or is happy with a current vendor. You don't get an opportunity to sell because the prospect can't see things your way.

For example, if a prospect doesn't see the value your products or services can add, she might say, "Your price is 15 percent

---

Sales Professional's Hot Tip #9

Invest Your Time. Average salespeople are *busy* during the course of the day. Successful sales professionals are both busy and *effective* during the course of the day. One of the keys to effectiveness is *investing* time being proactive rather than *spending* time being reactive.

Such sales professionals believe that they are the CEO and major stockholder in a franchise called "Me, Inc." They recognize time is the greatest asset they possess. The tools or resources they use to maximize their return on this asset are goals and priorities.

How can you possibly maximize your time without clearly defined goals and priorities? You can't. With so many things to do each day, the only way you can decide which are the most important is to develop clear goals.

Remember: It's not how busy we are but what we actually accomplish that counts most. If you focus on your goals, your activities will be much easier to prioritize.

---

higher. I'm sorry, but I don't see how your company is worth an extra 15 percent."

You say:

I can understand your desire not to pay higher prices than necessary these days. [*Supporting statement.*]

Suppose you were building a new home. [*Analogy.*]

I think you'd agree that the lowest price is not always the best deal. You'd want to work with a builder who had an excellent reputation for using high-quality materials and excellent craftsmanship at a fair price. Then we'd be talking about *value* instead of the lowest price. [*Analogy Reframe.*]

How important is it for your people to work with a company where high-quality, reliable products are the standard? A company that's committed to providing your people the "best value" in terms of:

1. Proven and reliable state-of-the-art products to maximize

performance and increase your productivity.

2. Compatible migration to new products in the future to protect your investment.

3. Reliable documentation and training to simplify use, minimize support, and cut overhead.

Which of these important issues should we talk about first to help increase your sales and profits? [*Analogy Reframe.*]

Note that we have reframed the discussion from "you're 15 percent higher" to the most "value" in terms of the three items mentioned above.

The 'Big Picture' Reframe

The second method is the "Big Picture" Reframe. This technique broadens the prospect's view to encompass a bigger picture. Your discussion moves from narrow concerns to larger issues (benefits) that will interest the customer. This gives you a chance to change his perspective.

Best Tip
Reframe prospects' concerns to both open their minds to new ideas and to emphasize value over price.

Let's deal with the price objection again. Prospect: "Your price is 15 percent higher. I'm sorry, but I don't see how you're worth it." You:

I understand your concern to get the best deal for your company. [*Supporting Statement.*] And that concern sounds like you're interested in the best value.

Let's talk about the best value for a minute in terms of:

Proven and reliable state-of-the-art products to maximize performance and increase productivity;

Compatible migration to new products in the future to protect your investment;

Reliable documentation and training to simplify use, minimize support, and cut overhead.

Which of these important issues should we talk about first to help increase your sales and profits? [*"Big Picture" Reframe.*]

Reframe by Bringing Up Key Benefits

Value

List three value-added benefits:

1. _____

2. _____

3. _____

Price

When they talk price, you reframe their thinking to incorporate value. How? By bringing up the three value-added benefits you've identified that address their concerns.

Note that we haven't started an argument with the customer over price. And we didn't imply the prospect was dumb because he forgot that high-quality, proven, state-of-the-art products maximize the company's performance. Or that compatible migration to new platforms in the future increases productivity. Or that reliable documentation simplifies use and minimizes support costs that cut overhead.

But we reminded him of all these things at a key moment. Success allows us to continue to sell.

Rather than lower your price, you've reframed the discussion to include the value-added benefits that are important to the prospect.

Remember: You don't want to lose the sale or lower your price. You want to open the customer's mind to the added value your firm provides.

Sales professionals earn their pay by reframing the customer's objections (price or anything else) so they can see the value-added benefits your solution offers.

Giftware arrived for the meeting on Friday. The group included three people, including their v.p. of operations.

The sales team's strategy: The first portion of the meeting was a review of the new systems to be announced later in the year. The second part would be an attempt to reframe their thinking so they thought "value" instead of "price."

The setting was the Executive Conference Center with its large, plush leather chairs, beautiful mahogany conference table, and Lenox china cups and saucers.

After some opening remarks, the Agile Manager turned the program over to the product-marketing manager to review the new products.

There was not much interest from the guests and very few questions.

Then it was the senior account manager's turn. Sarah thanked them all for coming and then asked a question. "Do you remember when we first talked about your situation and needs?"

They nodded their heads in agreement.

"We asked, 'Why do your customers do business with you.' Remember?"

They nodded.

Next, she reached under the podium and put two plastic bowls on top. She said, "The bowl on the right is made by Giftware. It holds three quarts, comes with a lid, and sells for $10. The bowl on the left is another brand. It also holds three quarts, comes with a lid, and sells for $6. Could one of you please tell me why the Giftware bowl is $4 higher than the other?" With that she folded her hands in front of her, smiled at the group and began looking each person in the eye.

An eerie silence fell over the room. It seemed to last for several minutes. In reality it was only a few seconds, but it required great courage for Sarah to stand in front of the group waiting for a response.

The v.p. of operations sat stone-faced with his arms folded.

Then, one of the Giftware people started to rock in his chair. He was about twenty-seven years old, and he could not stand the silence.

"They're not the same," said the young man.

The v.p. of operations turned quickly and glared at the young man with a laser-like stare.

"Oh?" said Sarah. "They look the same to me. How are they different?"

"Well, the Giftware bowl is manufactured to very high-quality specifications. It carries a lifetime guarantee, and it is sold by a direct sales organization." With each word the young man sank lower and lower into his chair, wishing he had remained silent.

Sarah spoke quickly. "So if I understand you, the Giftware product stands for high quality, is sold by a professional sales organization, and will last a lifetime. The other is a poor imitation, sold in any discount store, and will not last a lifetime. Is that about right?"

"Yes," said the young man very softly.

Sarah continued, "Let me ask you another question then, gentlemen. Since Giftware stands for high quality, service, and exceptional value, what message do you send your sales organization when you ask them to sell a premium product—but when you send them tools to do their job, you send a lower-priced imitation?"

Silence again engulfed the room.

Now the v.p. of operations broke the silence. "You must know your system was our first choice. We found it hard to justify the premium price to our senior management."

"Superior products, built to high quality standards, sold and supported by a top-notch organization, will always carry a premium price," said Sarah. "We call that *value*, and you folks certainly understand value."

The room once again became very quiet.

The Agile Manager spoke, "My, my look at the time. It's nearly noon. Let's move to our Executive Dining Room. After lunch, we'd like to review some financial options that we feel would benefit your company."

The v.p. of operations said, "We really would prefer to go with your company. Let's see if we can work this out."

As they walked toward the Executive Dining Room, the Agile Manager thought, What a great example of an Analogy Reframe. Value is defined by many things. Relating value to a prospect's business or products seems to work all the time.

A smile came across his face as he thought about the very professional job Sarah just did. She was able to open closed minds to see things from a different perspective in just five minutes. Life was good!

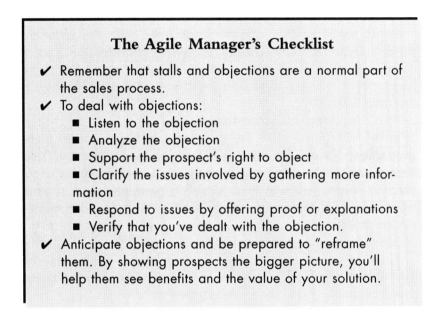

The Agile Manager's Checklist

✔ Remember that stalls and objections are a normal part of the sales process.

✔ To deal with objections:
- Listen to the objection
- Analyze the objection
- Support the prospect's right to object
- Clarify the issues involved by gathering more information
- Respond to issues by offering proof or explanations
- Verify that you've dealt with the objection.

✔ Anticipate objections and be prepared to "reframe" them. By showing prospects the bigger picture, you'll help them see benefits and the value of your solution.

Chapter Seven

Negotiate A Win-Win Agreement

Steve, a promising young sales rep, asked the Agile Sales Manager to accompany him to a meeting with a large customer. Steve had proposed a customized solution to this account, and he received word from his contact there that it had been approved by the executive v.p. All that remained was to work out the details of the contract.

The meeting was with a procurement manager from the customer's corporate headquarters. Steve had not met this person before.

When Steve and the Agile Manager arrived for the appointment, they signed in at the reception desk and waited for the procurement manager to come to the lobby. The procurement manager, Jim, soon greeted them. They exchanged pleasantries as they walked to a simply appointed conference room.

The Agile Manager sized up the man. His instincts told him that this was a mid-level procurement manager, probably with limited authority. Many large companies, he knew, used such individuals as their first level of contact for large contracts.

Jim offered coffee and cold drinks before they got down to business. As they drank their refreshments, Jim said there were only a few minor points that needed to be resolved.

Steve said, "That's great. I know a lot of your people are already clamoring for the implementation of the products and services we'll provide."

Steve had created a great deal of excitement. From the executive v.p. to individual department managers, people wanted the solution Steve had proposed. They were sold!

This only heightened Steve's excitement for the contract. His face said, "I want this deal and I want it today!"

The Agile Manager knew Jim was not as emotionally involved as Steve. He couldn't be. That was his job. His job was to get the most favorable deal for his company. He also, no doubt, wanted to prove his value to his company. That's code for cutting a better deal, and to many procurement people that means

---

Sales Professional's Hot Tip #10

Set Goals. Wise people have said, "Time waits for no one," "To waste time is to waste life," and "Time is the stuff life is made of."

If you look around, you'll see many people acting as though life is a dress rehearsal. To reach your goals, it is important to be satisfied with the way you distribute your time in each area of your life.

These different areas include family, social, professional, health, and spiritual. It's important to have balance; each area has an impact on another.

You'll enhance your chances of obtaining what you really want if you:

- Commit to goals by writing them down.

- Are as specific as possible.

- Set a deadline for each goal.

- Measure your progress.

- Aim high but realistically.

- Include long-, medium-, and short-range goals.

one thing: negotiate a lower price.

The Agile Manager watched and listened as Jim politely explained that the most important issue to resolve was the price.

"And we have a problem with the price you're quoting for your product," said Jim.

"But the executive v.p. said our price was OK," protested Steve. "We agreed on it. I thought we had a deal. What do you mean?"

"What I mean," said Jim tersely, "is that you don't have any deal unless I agree on the price."

"What's wrong with our price?" asked Steve.

"We usually pay a much lower price than you've quoted for this," said Jim.

"How much lower?" asked Steve.

Jim stared at Steve and said, "Eighty percent lower."

"You can't be serious," said Steve vigorously. "This is a customized solution."

"In consideration of that, and your past efforts with our company," said Jim, "we would be willing to pay 50 percent of your quoted price."

"What?" exclaimed Steve. "You've got to be kidding me!"

The Agile Manager realized he'd better cool Steve off. "Could you give us a few minutes alone, please?"

"Of course," said Jim with a smirk. "Let's take a break. I'll go get us some more coffee."

After he had left the room, Steve asked, "What's wrong with this guy? I thought we had a deal."

"He's just doing his job," said the Agile Manager. "He's made us an extremely low offer, hoping we'll compromise at an amount lower than what the executive v.p. agreed to."

"But why?" asked Steve.

"Because if he can negotiate a lower price, he has added value and he looks good to his superiors. In his mind, you have to understand, this is not a customized solution. This is a commodity purchase—like buying paper clips or ball-point pens," said the Agile Manager.

"What should we do?" asked Steve.

"I don't think we're negotiating at the right level," said the Agile Manager. "And we're at a disadvantage without a representative from the executive v.p.'s office—someone who wants to see this deal go through. I think we should close this meeting and ask for another session with all the interested parties."

"Can we do that?" asked Steve.

"Yes, we can," said the Agile Manager.

Jim returned with a freshly brewed pot of coffee. "Would you like cream and sugar?" he asked.

"No, thank you," said the Agile Manager. "I believe we are at an impasse. I suggest we set up another meeting with your executive vice president."

"What? I'm supposed to work this out with you," said Jim.

"I'm sorry," said the Agile Manager. "We don't feel this is a 'win-win' discussion. Thank you for your time." With that, Steve and the Agile Manager closed their notebooks and left the conference room.

"Hey, where are you going?" asked Jim.

"We're going back to our office," said Steve. "Have a good day."

Negotiating is a basic means of getting what you want from others. It's also a means for others to get what they want from you.

Put another way, negotiating is a communication process that allows you and your customer to reach agreement. It assumes that you and the customer have common interests and would like to reach agreement on certain issues.

These issues normally involve the terms and conditions under which you two will do business. They include pricing, support levels, training, upgrades, renewals, guarantees, payment schedules, and more.

| Best Tip

Don't glamorize or fear negotiating. It's nothing more than the process you use to reach agreement with another.

Strive for Win-Win Agreements

Win-win agreements are the best for all concerned.

A win-win sales negotiation is an agreement that is equally beneficial to both sides. The buyer and the seller come out of a negotiation with a workable agreement they can both live with and feel good about. When this occurs, lasting relationships develop that benefit both sides. Anything less usually spells trouble down the road.

Achieving win-win agreements is the challenge facing many sales professionals today. Salespeople sometimes approach a negotiation from a defensive position. They believe the other side is trying to squeeze them or take advantage of them. They end up compromising on a preferred position to get the business. Negotiations like this, with an adversarial cloud hanging over them, usually end up win/lose.

> **Best Tip**
>
> Take a customer-focused approach to sales. There's less chance the prospect will try to squeeze you on price or terms.

Salespeople who have taken a customer-focused approach through the sales process won't feel defensive at this point. They have laid the foundation of credibility and trust upon which to build a win-win negotiation. They know they can provide real value and thus have no need to feel defensive.

On the other hand, if salespeople haven't taken a customer-focused sales approach, then they may feel defensive due to a lack of confidence in the proposed solution. That defensiveness may lead to the very thing they fear—getting squeezed.

Basic Negotiation Strategies

Salespeople negotiate almost every day. They negotiate with prospects and customers. They negotiate with their "significant other" about where to have dinner, or what movie to see. Some even negotiate with a child at bedtime. Negotiation is a basic fact of life. Even though we may do it every day, it takes practice to do it well.

Let's take a look at some common strategies for negotiating:

1. Positional Negotiation Strategy. Each side takes a position and argues for it. Then both make concessions to reach agreement.

2. Hard Negotiation Strategy. Here, both sides take extreme positions. The negotiator who holds out longer wins.

3. Soft Negotiation Strategy. The negotiator wants to avoid personal conflict, so he makes concessions easily to reach agreement.

4. Win-Win Negotiation Strategy. Neither too hard nor too soft. Both sides avoid taking a fixed position, and they look for mutual gains whenever possible. Conflicts of interest are resolved fairly to both sides. Win-win agreements allow both buyer and seller to obtain what they want fairly and without either side caving in.

The Problem with a Positional Strategy

In positional negotiating, sides tend to lock in over positions and then compromise. But if the one side starts at an extreme position, the resulting compromise may be unattractive to the other. For example:

<u>Buyer:</u> For us to go with your company, we'd want a contract that locks in prices with no increases for five years.

<u>Seller:</u> We've never done that. My manager would immediately reject that.

<u>Buyer:</u> Look, you approached us. We are quite happy with your competitor. Do you want us to buy from your company or not?

<u>Seller:</u> Of course I do. Give me a day to talk to my manager. I'll see what we can do.

Depending how committed a buyer is to an extreme position, three things can happen:

1. The seller makes the concession.

2. Both sides make concessions. Usually, the seller makes the greater concession.

3. Neither side makes any concession, and therefore no deal is made.

In the example above, the buyer may be more committed to his or her position than the seller. The harder you try to get the buyer to compromise, the more committed she becomes. The egos of the individuals involved in the negotiation may get in the way, which makes it impossible to negotiate a fair agreement that everyone feels good about.

The Problem with Hard or Soft Negotiations

Either hard or soft negotiations can be damaging to a long-term business relationship. The hard negotiator wants to win for his side without regard for the other. He establishes a take-it-or-leave-it position and, unlike most positional negotiators, has no plan to compromise. The goal is to gain all concessions from the other side.

Best Tip

Never try to 'win' a negotiation using hardball tactics. It's a poor basis for initiating a business relationship.

In hard negotiations, feelings will probably get hurt, and concessions may be difficult to live with over the long haul. One or both participants will feel exhausted and beat up by the end.

You will encounter hard negotiators when you don't use a customer-focused sales approach.

Soft negotiations are nonconfrontational but produce the same one-sided agreements. People are less exhausted, but when one side gets the better of the deal, the agreement may be difficult or impossible to live with down the road. Negotiating a deal softly today and then hoping to improve it later may be difficult to accomplish. It may even open the door for the competition.

Naturally, variations of the hard and soft strategies exist. They involve a trade-off between getting what you want in a business sense, and getting along with people in a relationship or personal sense.

The Best: Win-Win Negotiations

Win-win negotiations are the only kind that result in beneficial contracts and deals for everyone involved.

Let the other side know right away that you are a win-win negotiator. Explain your strategy. Talk about the benefits to both of you from this approach. This type of negotiation will produce a satisfactory agreement for both sides, and in a style that will leave both parties satisfied.

Best Tip

Negotiate the most satisfactory deal you can *today*. Don't think you can 'improve' it a few months down the road.

Win-win negotiating requires:

1. Understanding people and getting an agreement that win-win relationships are fair and good business over the long haul.

2. Understanding the other side's interests—both business and personal.

3. Exploring and inventing options with the customer. For example, brainstorming several options that make sense.

4. Finding mutual satisfaction. What do both parties want? What constitutes a win for each?

On the way back to the office, the Agile Manager and Steve developed their plan of action.

Since the executive v.p. represented the end-user department, he needed to be informed of the meeting with Jim. He probably was unaware that a price negotiation was in progress.

Then, they agreed, they needed to get that executive or one of his people involved in the negotiation.

When they got back to the office, Steve called the executive v.p. Just as the Agile Manager had predicted, the executive v.p. was not aware of the price negotiation.

"I'm very sorry that this happened," he said. "We are usually more professional than this. I will call the person in charge of corporate procurement right now and arrange another meeting."

Steve asked, "Would it be possible for you to sit in?"

"I'm leaving this afternoon for a four-day trip to five different cities, replied the executive v.p. "I'll ask my director of operations to sit in on the meeting."

"That's great!" said Steve. "Do you want me to follow up?"

"Give me an hour, then call my director of operations. It's Carla Boskin. Do you have her number?"

"Yes, I do," said Steve. "Thanks for taking the time for this."

"It's no trouble. Your solution is exactly what we want. I'm sorry Jim was trying to squeeze you."

Later that afternoon, Steve called Carla Boskin. They scheduled another meeting for the following morning. Carla would indeed attend it herself, representing both the executive v.p. and the v.p. of corporate procurement.

Steve went to the Agile Manager's office with the news immediately. "Can you come to the meeting?" asked Steve.

"I wouldn't miss it," replied the Agile Manager. "We've got work to do if this is going to be a 'win-win' negotiation."

Just before a win–win negotiation, it's important to brainstorm a list of the issues that will be important to both sides. That'll help you plan a winning strategy.

For example, in the story above, Steve and the Agile Manager might brainstorm a list—based on information gathered in customer-focused interviews—like the one on the top of the next page.

Once you've completed that list, print two copies of it—one for you and one for your potential customer. Once in the negotiation, you'll show them your list and gain agreement that these are, indeed, the critical issues. The customer can add or delete items on the list or rearrange the order of priority.

Plan to Be Creative

In a win–win negotiation, it's almost always necessary to create solutions that satisfy the needs of both sides. To do that you

CUSTOMER ISSUES

✔ Increase Productivity
✔ Gain a Competitive
   Advantage
✔ Grow Market Share

✔ Adhere to Company
   Guidelines
✔ Show Value for the
   Investment

OUR ISSUES

✔ Satisfy Customer Needs
✔ Develop a Reference
   Account
✔ Adhere to Standard
   Pricing Practices
✔ Close the Business This
   Month
✔ Develop a Strong Rela-
   tionship

Before a negotiation, list issues important to each side.

must know what you and the customer want.

This includes both business and personal interests. You're at a disadvantage if you don't know the customer's personal win (or dream). Remember: The customer knows that your win is usually tied to some financial reward.

When you have a clear understanding of prospects' interests, identify, rank, and explain yours. Allow them to ask questions to help them understand your situation.

Together, analyze both lists of interests:

- Which items are most important and why?
- What are areas of common interest?
- Where are your interests opposed?
- What are the financial considerations (both immediate and long term)?

Explore and Invent Options

Unless each side understands well the interests of the other side, exploring and inventing win-win options is just not possible.

Be specific in what you want. In addition, have some possible options to reach the win-win in mind. The overall tone of the negotiation is usually set by the extent that you have prepared possible options in advance. Preparing allows you to "seed" the negotiation with possibilities.

Don't limit your thinking to solutions that have worked in the past. Get creative. Invent new options if you don't like the old ones or if the old options won't make the situation win-win.

Be careful, however. Don't re-write company policy and pro-cedures. On the contrary, propos-ing something new without the prior approval of your manager can be disastrous. You may not be able to deliver on a promise!

*B*est *T*ip
Don't let your creativity get you in trouble. Check with higher-ups to make sure you can deliver on promises.

Always check with your manager first. If he or she can't pro-vide you with approval for an option, brainstorm together for one that would be approved.

To invent new options:

1. Define the problem. Get the facts: details, people involved, special situations, etc.

2. Diagnose the problem. Divide it into smaller pieces.

3. See what's missing and what may have caused the prob-lem. Analyze the situation.

4. Develop (brainstorm) new approaches for mutual gain.

5. Assign action items for both parties to test the feasibility of a new option.

Whatever you do:

- Don't make an early judgment on a single option.
- Don't stop inventing new options after only one.
- Don't assume the answer is fixed. Expand your thinking.
- Don't use options that serve only your interests.
- Don't be afraid to brainstorm with associates and the customer.

Find the Win-Win

Use a white board flip chart, or just a note pad, and list the possible options. Ask your customer to add to your list of options, or develop new options together. All that matters is that you consider both of your interests.

Once you have brainstormed several options that you believe get you and the prospect what you want, you're halfway there. Now you need to find which option is the best for both of you.

As ever, get prospects' input, ideas, and feelings. Allow them to select the best option that satisfies the needs and interests of you both.

The following morning, Steve and the Agile Sales Manager were in the lobby of the customer's building ten minutes before the scheduled meeting. They were greeted by Carla Boskin and the director of procurement, a man named Mel. Missing was Jim, whom they had met with the day before.

As they walked to the conference room, Steve asked, "Where is the procurement manager we met with yesterday?"

"Oh, he's busy on another project," said Mel. "He won't be at this meeting."

Sales Professional's Hot Tip #11

Stay Focused and Set Priorities. After setting goals, decide which activities must be done to reach them. Then prioritize those activities in the order they must be done.

Picture your long-range goals everyday to help maximize your effectiveness and get your top priorities accomplished. Ask yourself, "Is this activity going to move me closer to achieving my goal?" If the answer is "no," switch to an activity that will help you achieve your goal.

Important projects and activities help you achieve your goals. Sometimes things that appear urgent may not be important.

Steve smiled to himself and thought, One for us.

Mel opened the meeting, "I hope a reasonable agreement can be reached. The executive v.p. called me yesterday and spoke very highly about your customized solution. He said it would help increase productivity."

Steve smiled and said, "We hope we can work things out. A lot of effort by many people has gone into this project."

The Agile Manager said, "I believe we all want a long-term relationship. We would like to discuss an agreement that is win-win."

"Win-win agreements are the best in the long run," agreed Mel. "We'd been discussing that before you arrived."

"Good," said the Agile Manager. "This is an important project for both of our companies. I hope we'll be giving each other 'high fives' after we work it out."

Mel looked directly at the Agile Manager and said, "High fives? I've never done high fives with a supplier." Then with a smile he said, "That would be really novel!"

For the next two and a half hours the group negotiated. Steve began by echoing the Agile Manager: "We like to negotiate win-win agreements. Then we have a process for doing business that is fair and that will produce the results we all expect. Does that seem reasonable?"

They all nodded in agreement. This was the first critical step in the negotiation—gaining the customer's commitment to negotiate a win-win.

Steve distributed copies of the "Important Issues" worksheet. He read them off one by one and asked Mel and Carla to confirm the importance of each.

Mel said, "These look very good. What do you mean by 'standard pricing practices'?"

Steve said, "We have quoted you our standard pricing for the quantity and time frame we've proposed."

"Can you do better than that?" asked Mel.

"If we increase the quantity and extend the time, you would be entitled to a greater discount. That's our standard pricing policy," said the Agile Manager.

Carla added, "Well, our plan is to implement your solution in North America first, and if we achieve the results we expect, we will implement it in Europe, South America, Asia, and Australia next year."

Mel said, "That volume would be significantly greater than North America alone."

"Yes, it would," said Carla.

"May I make a suggestion?" asked the Agile Manager. All eyes turned toward him. "Why don't you folks run the numbers to determine what the total volume would be worldwide. We'll make a phone call to get approval for an additional discount based on the increased quantity. I think we'll be able to quote you firm pricing for the next twenty-four months. Does that make sense?"

Best Tip

Research issues you know will come up in the negotiation. Ask yourself, 'What is likely to concern them the most?'

With that, Carla and Mel left the meeting to discuss the issue.

The win-win negotiation was going very well. Steve estimated the increased quantity would be two and a half times the original number. This was Steve's entire quota for the year!

The Agile Manager telephoned his office to get approval for an additional discount based on quantity. The manager in charge of pricing wanted to know if this would be a "firm" contract or a blanket order. With a blanket order, the customer is not required to take the quantity. It is only an estimate and does not receive as great a discount level. This was standard pricing policy.

The Agile Manager asked for discounts based on firm contract pricing.

When the group resumed the negotiation, Carla said, "We've just spoken with our executive v.p. He said based on a successful implementation in North America, the quantity for the other areas would be increased by a factor of three."

Steve thought, Triple the volume!

Sales Professional's Hot Tip #12

Invest in Self-Improvement. Studying your business and improving your skills are like placing money in the bank, investing in your future. Therefore:

1. Add continuously to your resources of knowledge and skills. Take classes, read sales books, and—especially—learn from your fellow salespeople. Each has unique insights that will help you sell better.

2. Listen to self-improvement, sales, and motivational tapes when driving.

3. Never pass up an opportunity to develop yourself by taking on new tasks, joining others on special projects, or volunteering to go after the known "difficult sell." When the boss asks for volunteers, make sure your hand goes into the air first.

When you're determined to improve your selling skills, you will.

Mel then asked, "What did your people say?"

The Agile Manager spoke. "We asked for pricing for two and three times the original quantity. Here are our best figures for a firm contract over a two-year period."

Mel and Carla looked at the discount structure. They asked if they could be excused for a few minutes once again. As they left the room, Steve looked at the Agile Manager and said, "What do you think?"

The Agile Manager said, "I think they're okay on the discount level. They may have a problem with the firm contract."

"What can we do if they ask us for the discount without the firm contract?" asked Steve.

"We've negotiated fairly with them. It's their job to ask us if this is our best offer. I believe it is," said the Agile Manager.

Moments later, the two rejoined Steve and the Agile Manager.

The director of procurement took the lead role. "Is this your most favored pricing for quantities of 3,000?"

"Yes, it is," said the Agile Manager.

"We're satisfied that this is your best price, and we think it is fair. Frankly, we have a problem with that quantity over twenty-four months. We'd be more comfortable if we had thirty months to complete the implementation."

Steve looked at the Agile Manager and said, "We can do that, can't we?"

The Agile Manager smiled and said, "My people have given me the authority to extend that pricing to you for up to thirty-six months. You see, we want this solution to be implemented successfully. We're in this for the long haul and if six additional months will make you more comfortable, then so be it."

Best Tip

Understand that negotiating a large contract requires great perseverance. It can take months to seal the deal.

"Then I think we have our win-win agreement," said Mel. "I'll have a purchase order cut right away. I'll be back in ten minutes."

He returned with the P.O. for almost triple the original deal. This contract could make Steve the number one salesperson in the country!

Both Steve and the Agile Manager soaked up the moment.

To a sales professional, there is no greater feeling than negotiating and closing a large win–win contract.

It's always the culmination of many months of hard work:

- Meetings with all the key people to identify needs, goals, priorities, and the personal win.
- Crafting a unique customer-focused solution to meet the customer's needs.
- Demonstrating that the company can implement the solution and provide the support services to keep things running smoothly.

Only then does the customer company receive the value it was looking for in the first place. Only then is it truly a win–win.

Mel returned with the signed purchase order. Everybody smiled and shook hands.

As the Agile Manager and Steve were walking out of the conference room, Mel said, "Hey, wait a minute. You forgot something. What about the high fives?"

The Agile Manager flashed a huge smile as he and Steve high-fived their way out the door. Life is good!

Prepare to Negotiate: Final Tips

1. **Know what you want.** Know what you want the deal to look like after the negotiation. Specifically, what will make this a fair deal for you and your company?

2. **Know what they want.** Conduct your customer-focused interviews with all the other side's key influencers and decision makers.

3. **Do your homework.** Research answers to the important issues involved in this negotiation in advance. Consider the important questions and concerns your prospect will have.

4. **Know what the win-win looks like.** Determine how you can satisfy what your prospect is looking for and what you and your company are looking for.

5. **Consider other contingencies:**

■ Have you considered the needs of all of the interested parties to the negotiation?

■ What is the time limit on the negotiation, if any?

■ Who would like to keep things as they are, who wants the change and why?

■ What does a delay cost the prospect and you? Who will be involved in the final negotiation?

6. **Practice the negotiation.** Practicing prior to the actual negotiation makes for a smoother delivery on your part. By role playing the negotiation in a safe environment ahead of time, you can polish your exchange and be prepared.

The Agile Manager's Checklist

✔ Of the four common negotiating strategies—positional, hard, soft, and win-win—only win-win sets the foundation for a long-term business relationship.

✔ To negotiate successfully:
- Agree to aim for a win-win deal;
- Understand the other side's interests;
- Explore and invent options with the customer;
- Satisfy the interests of both sides.

✔ To ease negotiations, identify, rank, and explain your interests for the benefit of the customer.

✔ Plan to be creative. It's a rare win-win that doesn't require brainstorming new options.

✔ Practice the negotiation beforehand. You'll achieve a smoother delivery.

Chapter Eight

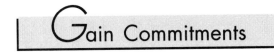

Gain Commitments

Closing a sale usually requires the salesperson to make many "little closes" along the way. We call these "commitments to action." They serve as a strong indication that the prospect is interested in your solution.

Getting prospects to agree to meet you for a customer-focused interview, for example, is a little commitment. Getting them to let you speak with other people inside their organization is a little commitment. Getting decision makers to agree that you can satisfy their needs is a greater commitment.

Get enough of these little commitments, and it puts you in position to ask for the big commitment, the contract or purchase order. And that's the logical conclusion to all that you have done to that point.

You probably obtained business in the past, for example, without actually asking for the order. This often occurs when you've done the right things along the way.

Start to Close at the Beginning

"Closing the sale is a process, not a point in time," said NCR's Dick Gately.

Closing actually begins the very first time you speak with a prospect. The prospect decides to continue the discussion or to cut it off. The decision-making process continues throughout the entire sales process.

Think about the decisions (commitments) that prospects will make in the sales process.

Little commitments include:

- Agreeing to speak with you on the phone.
- Meeting with you or someone else in person.
- Allowing you to conduct a customer-focused interview.
- Assisting you in gathering information.
- Taking you on a tour of their facility.

Bigger commitments include:

- Explaining current problems and future requirements to you.
- Describing plans, priorities, goals, and dreams to you.
- Calling one of your customers for a reference.
- Agreeing that your solution or proposal will satisfy their needs.

Final commitments include:

- Buying your solution or product.
- Writing a testimonial letter for you.
- Recommending you and your company to others.

Adopt a Winning Attitude

Your success in gaining both small and large commitments is a direct result of your skill and attitude. You need good sales skills to get in to see prospects, qualify them, and then gather the information necessary to make customer-focused presentations.

Your success in closing the sale is greatly enhanced when you improve your attitude. If you don't believe that your company is the best, why should the prospect? Remove any doubt from your mind and replace it with a positive expectation of success. You must convey to your prospects and customers that they will

---

Sales Professional's Hot Tip #13

Set Goals to Avoid Procrastinating. Procrastination is something that we are all potentially vulnerable to. Procrastinators often perform low-priority activities instead of more important ones. To avoid wasting time:

- Take the suggestions on goal setting (page 79) to heart.

- Take action and commit to your goals in writing.

- Prioritize the activity that must be done to realize your goals.

Many people procrastinate because they lack goals and priorities. As a result, they may in fact be putting off unimportant activities and yet worrying about them needlessly. But you'll never know until you decide what you should be doing when you get out of bed each day.

---

benefit from doing business with you and your company. You need to be poised, relaxed, and confident.

Worried about your poise? From years of experience, we can assure you that you will be poised, relaxed, and confident when you follow the customer-focused selling process. Having earned the trust and confidence of your prospects makes it easy for them to open up and share their needs, issues, goals, and personal wins.

That clear understanding allows you to create a solution that helps them get what they want. Why would you be any less than full of poise and confidence at this point?

Ask for the Order

Volumes have been written on asking for the order. Most of these techniques are not suited for professionals selling business solutions and support services. That's because most rely on "outsmarting" the prospect. More important than closing the sale, to the sales professional, is gaining or keeping the customer.

And you can forget about needing to ask for the order three, four, or five times, as so many "experts" recommend. If you have followed the customer-focused sales system up to this point, you will usually ask for the order only once. And you will get it. Why? Because you are helping people get what they want, and you are assisting in the decision process.

The following techniques are all you need to ask for the order successfully.

1. The Direct Close

The direct close is best used when you have encountered little or no resistance. It will be well received by most prospects. It is the logical conclusion to all previous selling activities.

Examples:

"Are you ready to proceed?"

"Can you issue the purchase order today?"

"Will you give me the go-ahead today?"

"If you sign today, we can begin the installation immediately."

2. The Assumptive/Indirect Close

This close begins with a conversational statement that assumes you have the order and asks an indirect question about schedules, colors, configurations, etc. A positive response means your prospect has bought.

Examples:

"The productivity of your people should really improve with the new system. When were you thinking you'd want to start?"

Best Tip

When you gain enough little commitments, ask for the big one—the contract or order.

"A year from now, Bob, you'll be pleased you selected us for this project. You'll like the way your people can access inventory files in the stores, and you'll see the difference that makes to your retail customers. Shall we look at the contract?"

3. The Positive-Choice Close

This is a variation of the assumptive/indirect close. It begins conversationally and offers your prospect a choice of two or three solutions, all of them positive. This is an effective close when dealing with domineering personalities, who like making decisions and being in control.

Example:

"Mr. Harris, we'd like you to decide how to establish control

> **|Best Tip**
>
> Use the Direct Close when prospects have shown little or no resistance. They should be receptive.

and administer the roll-out of products. Purchasing can maintain tight control or you could elect to keep other functional responsibilities at the departmental level. Which way would you like to begin?"

4. The "Ben Franklin" Close

This is a decision-making process said to have originated with Benjamin Franklin. Whenever old Ben was faced with a difficult decision, he would draw a large "T" on a piece of paper. On one side of the T, he would write REASONS FOR. On the opposite side he would write REASONS AGAINST. Then he wrote down all the reasons for and against a particular decision. After studying both sides of the T, he would make his decision.

You can adapt this same approach to some of your business situations. All behavior styles (see pages 65–68 for a refresher) will allow you to summarize the important benefits that your approach provides.

By using a list of the reasons for (your benefits) and the reasons against (include some of your competition's advantages), you can help your prospect draw the proper conclusion. By listing some reasons for hesitation, you will also add to your credibility and trustworthiness.

If the pluses don't outweigh the minuses, you are probably

trying to get a decision prematurely. You may need to gather more information about the needs, goals, priorities, and personal win. Example:

REASONS FOR	REASONS AGAINST
1. Increased productivity	1. Learning curve
2. Gain a competitive advantage	2. Fear of change by some
3. Grow market share	
4. Supports business plans	
5. Show value for the investment	

5. The Benefit-Summary Close

Some people will want you to summarize the important benefits that your solution can provide them. When you receive favorable comments from your presentation and your trial closes are positive, a nice way to "wrap up" is with a benefit-summary close.

Example:

"Barbara, I think you'll agree that our approach will be an investment in success for your business. Let's review the key benefits you'll receive:

- Improved customer service. You'll improve customer service substantially by reducing order-fulfillment times.
- Improved productivity. This system reduces product handling, replenishment, and costly error.
- Lower maintenance costs. We offer a five-year warranty on all parts and labor.

What's our next step?"

6. The Critical Date/Tight Schedule Close

This close can be effective in situations where an upcoming event will change your offering. Sometimes you can use the critical date to create a sense of urgency with your prospect. But be careful and avoid bluffing. Otherwise it'll backfire on you.

And when dealing with a detail-oriented prospect, be certain you can provide logical proof.

Examples:

"Mary, we've just received word that a rate increase is going into effect the first of next month. I can lock you in at our original quotation if you give me the go-ahead this week. Are you in a position to act?"

"Pat, you've said you'd like to get started this quarter. Our training organization is telling me that it'll be fully scheduled by the end of next week. For us to meet your timetable, I'll need a signed contract by Friday. Will that be possible?"

7. The Turn-Around Close ("I Must Have Done Something Wrong")

There will be situations in which you put in the time and effort to provide a customer-focused solution. You prepared your recommendation and conducted a five-star presentation.

But when you ask for the order, you don't get an objection and you don't get a no. You get a stall of some sort or a "let me think it over."

To turn this situation around, you need to flush out the real reason for the delay. If you have established your trust and credibility, the following can work wonders.

"Mr. Jones, I understand. You want to make a sound decision.

Best Tip

Try the Turn-Around Close when you've conducted a superb customer-focused sales effort and you still get a stall.

I've studied your requirements and objectives, and I understand your concerns. So, please help me out. I must have done something wrong to leave you undecided. What did I miss?"

Naturally, if you have credibility and the prospect trusts you, you should always ask this question any time you learn of a decision to go with a competitor. If you believe in what you're doing, you owe it to the prospect as well as to yourself and your organization.

Sales Professional's Hot Tip #14

Analyze Opportunities. Evaluate your chances of making a sale realistically. Decide what the potential opportunity of an account is to you, and how much of your time will be required to close.

Ask yourself if this opportunity is worth more of your time. Could you spend your time more effectively by working on another account? If you're not sure, ask your manager or an associate. Don't chase your tail month after month. Life is too short.

If you're not going to close an account in a reasonable amount of time, drop it. Find another prospect, work on another deal, or turn it over to someone else. But don't beat a dead horse.

Once you learn the reasons, you have uncovered objections you can deal with. If the relationship is based on trust, you can often turn the situation around. Worst case, you've established something to build on in the future with this prospect as well as others.

Adapt Your Close to the Prospect

Remember how we classified buyers a few chapters back? You'll improve your success rate by adapting your style to the prospect during the close.

Dominance Style

Be concise and businesslike. Don't waste time with idle talk. Get to the points of interest quickly and summarize. Offer a choice or a decision to make.

Don't assume you have the order. Ask for a decision. Use either the direct close or the positive-choice close. After you ask for a decision, wait for an answer.

Influential Style

Eliminate the details. Just hit the high points. Visualize, through word pictures, what your "new approach" or "finished system" will look like. Talk about the results you will provide. Socialize. Talk about your follow-on support services and how good the buyer will look to other people in the organization.

Use the assumptive/indirect close to avoid a direct decision. These prospects will feel more comfortable with this approach. After asking a closing question, let the prospect answer.

Steadiness Style

Earn trust during your customer-focused interview, presentation, and other discussions. Be warm and friendly. Use trial closes to test the water regularly. Take it slow and easy. Be sure to answer all questions.

Use the "Ben Franklin" or benefit-summary close and get agreement that these are the most important benefits. If they stall, try the "I must have done something wrong turn-around." This will usually get hidden objections onto the table where you can deal with them. Again, after you ask your closing question, wait for an answer.

Conscientiousness Style

Don't rush the sales process. Be patient. Don't socialize or get "up close and personal." Back up the points they are interested in with facts and figures. Be sure you answer all questions before you ask for commitment.

Avoid the critical-date close. Use the "Ben Franklin" or benefit-summary close, but in greater detail. Offer proof of your claims. Expect them to ask more "why?" questions than the other types. Be steady and, especially, logical. Keep emotions out of this close. They don't work. Let them answer your questions.

Persevere and Persist

Many years ago, IBM's Thomas J. Watson, Sr., said, "Keep track of those people who say 'no,' because next week, next month, or next year they are going to say 'yes' to somebody who is selling your kind of product. Selling is a building proposition."

These words are just as true today. When a prospect doesn't buy your proposition today, follow up. Don't keep calling back to rehash what has already been discussed. Call back with new information, new developments, new ideas, or a new approach. Perseverance is the mark of a superior salesperson.

If you're having trouble, make sure you've done the essential things: create interest, develop trust, conduct a F.I.N.D. interview, present a customer-focused solution, handle objections, and gain commitments. If you feel you've missed a step, back up and start over. Are you speaking to the decision maker? Have you identified her needs and important issues? Did you uncover her goals and a personal win? If you haven't, find out what they are.

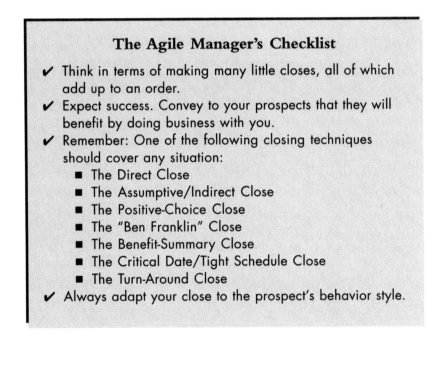

The Agile Manager's Checklist

✔ Think in terms of making many little closes, all of which add up to an order.

✔ Expect success. Convey to your prospects that they will benefit by doing business with you.

✔ Remember: One of the following closing techniques should cover any situation:

■ The Direct Close
■ The Assumptive/Indirect Close
■ The Positive-Choice Close
■ The "Ben Franklin" Close
■ The Benefit-Summary Close
■ The Critical Date/Tight Schedule Close
■ The Turn-Around Close

✔ Always adapt your close to the prospect's behavior style.

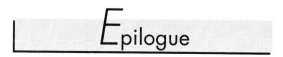

Epilogue

Early in his management career, the Agile Sales Manager worked for a small start-up computer company that was part of a larger corporation. Its charter was to sell products to the commercial marketplace.

In the first two years the company existed, the handful of people that made up the sales organization managed to grow the business slowly.

One day, the Agile Manager's lone sales rep for the East Coast came back from a swing through New England. He was updating the Agile Manager on his activity and pulled out a large three-ring binder that must have easily weighed ten pounds with all the paper in it.

He was very excited. He explained that he had heard about a pre-bid information conference that the military was holding. It involved a large purchase requirement.

The Agile Manager interrupted and said "We really have enough on our plate. Besides, that clearly doesn't involve commercial business."

"I know," said the salesperson. "But they say that there is potential here for $300 million worth of revenue over a three-year period! Won't you please see if senior management would let us take a run at this opportunity?"

The Agile Manager agreed. A few days later, he found himself in corporate headquarters explaining the situation to a senior executive who had strong opinions on just about everything and who made very quick decisions.

Cutting the Agile Manager off midstream, he said, "That's all well and good, but the opportunity you're proposing is outside the market we're targeting. I don't want you to pursue it any further."

With that he made it clear that the meeting was over, and the Agile Manager left. On the telephone that night, the Agile Manager told the salesperson to drop the idea of pursuing the military contract.

Roughly two weeks later, the same sales rep, wearing a sheepish grin on his face, approached the Agile Manager again. "I know you told me to back off that military opportunity," he said. "But I decided to invest another couple of hours at another meeting and I have great news. There were over two hundred companies—all potential competitors—at the first meeting. But there were only half that number at this conference!"

The Agile Manager chuckled to himself. He thought that maybe management in other organizations had given similar directions to their salespeople that were actually followed.

The sales rep's enthusiasm persuaded the Agile Manager to pursue the matter one more time with the organization's leader. An opportunity presented itself a few days later at headquarters as he was wrapping up a meeting on another topic.

"If you could give me five minutes," he said, "there is just one other thing I'd like to talk to you about."

"Sure," said the executive, "just as long as it has nothing to do with that military project we discussed the last time I saw you."

The Agile Manager grimaced but forged ahead. "It could put us in the black well ahead of schedule—"

"I'm sorry," said the executive curtly. "I have other things to attend to." He walked over to a file cabinet.

The Agile Manager rose glumly and headed for the door. But just as he was turning the doorknob, he stopped and did his best Lieutenant Columbo imitation.

Turning back toward the executive, he said, "As one of the four people you brought in to start this business, I'm sorry that I'm letting you down."

"What do you mean?" asked the exec. "Things are going fairly well. The board of directors is happy with the results that you've achieved so far."

Sitting back down, the Agile Manager said, "I'm glad to hear that. But I'm letting you down—as well as the organization—by not doing an effective job presenting a case for us pursuing this military opportunity. I'd really like to know what it is that I've done or not done that's preventing you from letting us compete for this business."

"Going after that business," said the executive, "will require a huge amount of time. And while that sales rep is chasing a contract that hundreds of other companies will also go after, he'll neglect the commercial accounts that we need to develop for long-term growth."

He wasn't through. "Just the administrative effort alone would be enormous—and with no guarantee of success."

"Thanks for clarifying your reasoning," said the Agile Manager. "Tell you what: I'll assume personal responsibility for the East Coast rep's quota. And we won't have to hire extra administrative help to work on the project. Tom Backov told me that some clerical people in the imaging division are twiddling their thumbs. He'd be happy to loan 'em to us for a few months."

The executive appeared to be giving careful thought to what he had heard.

The Agile Manager added, "Of course, I'm sure that the board of directors, as well as the stockholders, would be thrilled beyond belief to see a *Wall Street Journal* headline six months from now announcing that our small, start-up division won a contract valued at $300 million over a three-year period."

The Agile Manager hoped this had struck an emotional nerve. The division's revenue to that point was only a little over $50 million.

Rising from his chair, the executive stuck out his hand and shook the Agile Manager's hand warmly. "Go ahead with the first few steps in the project. We'll see where it might take us," he said. "Good Luck!"

Close to a year later, the Agile Manager felt somewhat like a prophet as he read the *Wall Street Journal* headline that announced the gigantic win for the organization.

The difference that the sales professional made in this situation (with the assistance of numerous other team members) was enormous. It turned out the contract was worth almost double what the estimate had been. Not bad for what was a tiny start-up company trying to find a place in a very competitive market.

In Conclusion . . .

Sometimes a sales professional can make a difference selling commodity items like bananas on a beach in the Caribbean. Sometimes a sales professional can impact an organization and the number of people it employs on a scale so vast that it's difficult to comprehend.

But as long as people buy from people, the sales professional will always make the difference.

Index

Among the Books in the Agile Manager Series™
At your bookseller, or call 888-805-8600 or visit
www.agilemanager.com

The Agile Manager's Guide To
GIVING GREAT PRESENTATIONS

By Jeff Olson

The Agile Manager's Guide To
EXTRAORDINARY CUSTOMER SERVICE

By Susan M. Gage

The Agile Manager's Guide To
GETTING ORGANIZED

By Jeff Olson

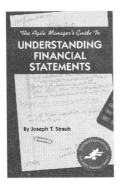

The Agile Manager's Guide To
UNDERSTANDING FINANCIAL STATEMENTS

By Joseph T. Straub

The Agile Manager's Guide To
BUILDING AND LEADING TEAMS

By Joseph T. Straub

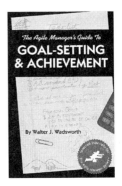

The Agile Manager's Guide To
GOAL-SETTING & ACHIEVEMENT

By Walter J. Wadsworth

The Agile Manager's Guide To
MANAGING IRRITATING PEOPLE

By Joseph T. Straub

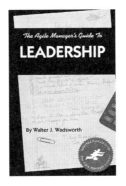

The Agile Manager's Guide To
LEADERSHIP

By Walter J. Wadsworth

The Agile Manager's Guide To
INFLUENCING PEOPLE

By John R. Hook